Trevor Wye

Proper Flute Playing

GW00535827

A Companion to the Practice Books

NOVELLO

This volume is companion to *A Practice Book for the Flute* by Trevor Wye (also available from Novello).

This highly successful series of Practice Books for the Flute has proved to be of tremendous value to players of all grades from beginners to advanced students. Each book has a dependence upon the others and concentrates in detail on an individual facet of flute playing. Collectively they form a broad reference to the technical difficulties of the instrument, without concentrating on any one particular method of study.

There are six volumes in the series:

A full list of Trevor Wye's Novello publications is printed at the end of this volume.

© Copyright 1988 Novello & Company Limited

No part of this publication may be copied or
reproduced in any form or by any means without the
prior permission of Novello & Company Limited

Printed in Great Britain

For Meg and David Mendel, ✶ *whose inspiration it was, with love*

CONTENTS

ACKNOWLEDGMENTS

The author wishes to record his grateful thanks to Dot, who made coffee, cooked meals and typed the script and to Russell Parry, Kate Hill and Clare Southworth who read the first draft and offered helpful advice and comment.

T.W. 1988

★Proper Doctoring by David Mendel, MB, FRCP (Springer-Verlag).

PREFACE

The large majority of flute players world-wide are women. To try to be non-partisan in the text, I adopted 'him or her' but found this to be much too fussy. I then alternated these references and kept count. That, too, was daft. Finally, I decided to adopt 'him'. It just might help to redress the balance! Anyway, it's a lot less fussy.

Much of the material of this book is based on personal experience and observation, and 'points' gained from my teachers. The number of words used in any section or subsection is, in my judgement, sufficient for clarity. If very few words are used to express an idea, this bears no relationship to the importance which I attach to it.

INTRODUCTION

Proper Flute Playing is concerned with the basic building blocks upon which to develop a firm control of the flute, a good technique and a beautiful tone. It is not intended to favour any particular 'school' of playing, as all schools ultimately point to the same goal: the beautiful performance of music. Most of the practical side of playing is detailed in my *Practice Books for the Flute* series, and it is not my intention to repeat that information again, except where it is necessary to amplify the points raised in those books. Almost all flute playing techniques are common sense. That is the basis on which this book has been written.

At the time of writing (1988) it is estimated that there are about 200,000 flute players in the United Kingdom alone. That's a lot of flute players. Why, then, aren't there relatively large numbers of brilliant virtuosi? The flute is an easy instrument requiring a certain talent, but with that number of players there should be many more brilliant performers than there are. We can speculate on the reason: a point is reached in a player's progress where the difficulties become too great. At that moment, a player's basic knowledge of the building blocks of flute playing is insufficient to carry him toward further progress.

Flute playing requires specific skills; they can be listed as the basic ingredients of Proper flute playing: determination and enthusiasm; physical fitness for the task; flexible fingers; a reasonable 'ear'; some intelligence; a good sense of rhythm; a 'feeling' for music; an aptitude for the flute. There are others, of course. An incapacity in any one of these areas will weaken the whole structure.

The acquisition of the skills required for Proper flute playing can be likened to building a house: first, the foundations need to be laid before the building of the supporting footings and pillars. Any weakness in the early stages will cause the structure to be unsound. The more advanced the building becomes, the less stable it will be if there is fundamental weakness which hasn't been rectified.

Many young players level off in their climb to acquire a good standard of performance because of one or more weaknesses in their basic technical skills. Possibly this is because they haven't been taught all of them; or possibly because they have chosen to ignore the advice of their teachers. This book will endeavour to simplify the learning of the basic skills required to be a Proper flute player.

FINDING A TEACHER

There are few *really* good teachers, just as there are few really good players, doctors, or car mechanics.

At school we remember the few really good teachers for most of our lives. We remember the subject taught by a *really* good teacher even if we have no natural ability in that subject. A really good teacher knows how to communicate knowledge, knows how to inspire, to interest his pupils. A really good teacher doesn't *learn* how: it is part of his personality to be like that. This is not to say that there are only a few really good teachers, and the remainder are no good. The number of good teachers, average teachers and below average teachers follows the same pattern of distribution as it does for doctors or car mechanics or the population in general. How to find a good one is the problem.

Junior Level: Although it's better to have a teacher who actually plays your instrument, this is by no means essential. The teacher should at least play a related woodwind instrument with some skill, but the most important gift of a Proper teacher is enthusiasm.

The flute was designed to be played in a particular way: it is hard to play it to the left side of your body with the blow-hole on your top lip. It wasn't designed to be played like that. Therefore, even if you were to pick up some faults, either through your own carelessness, or because your teacher doesn't care, it isn't very serious. The faults can be corrected. It is better not to acquire them in the first place, of course. Unlearning something and re-learning it are together much more difficult and time-consuming. But, if the choice of teacher in your locality is limited – perhaps limited to one – then you have no option. If there is a choice, telephone around. Somebody is sure to have heard about a good teacher. If a teacher is employed by a Local Education Authority, or a music school, it is no guarantee that he is competent. Some good teachers prefer to be independent. Enquire at local music shops, too. That can be a good source of information. The enthusiastic teacher should be well known at your local music shop.

Middle Level: If the flute is to be taken a little more seriously or you are dissatisfied with your present teacher, or you may have 'outgrown' him, then look around. County, and National College Saturday morning music schools may be the answer for those with more talent, though this again is no guarantee of excellent tuition. Many good teachers prefer to remain independent of these institutions. Saturday schools do offer a broad musical education, including orchestral experience and theory, and can offer an attractive and economical package for the more talented youngster.

Some young players won't know whether or not their teacher, or prospective teacher is in the 'really good' class. Here are some pointers. The pupils of a good teacher will be very enthusiastic about him and some will themselves play well, too. Ask at your local music shop and at school, in youth bands and orchestras.

If the choice of teachers locally is limited, then travel elsewhere for lessons, particularly if you are already reasonably advanced. A lesson of good quality every two or three weeks is worth more than a whole term of indifferent lessons. In fact, a term of indifferent lessons isn't worth anything.

A frequent cause for concern to parents is that a pupil may create bad feeling by changing to another teacher. This can indeed happen. But, on the other hand, a Proper pupil can, with tact and understanding, partly overcome this. Most teachers are used to pupils leaving, moving, or giving up. With an especially talented pupil, it may be hard for the teacher to accept, but a Proper teacher ought to be able to see that it will be in the interests of his pupil in the long term.

At the time of writing, the author believes there are fifteen or twenty 'really good' Proper flute teachers in the United Kingdom. And, this may surprise the reader, four of them are in London, while another five of them are *peripatetic* teachers; that's to say, not principal players in orchestras. Only three of them are full-time orchestral players.

Don't be misled. "I'm going to London (or New York) for lessons". So, who to? Alas, that often seems less important; "I'm going to London for lessons" – ipso facto, the lessons are sure to be a) excellent; b) the best available in the country; c) very expensive, and therefore excellent. What nonsense!

One of the best ways to find a good teacher is to attend a summer school where there are many flute players, perhaps fifty or more. Then ask around and observe. Don't worry if the most recommended teacher is one you haven't heard of before. The best teachers don't always appear on television, or make gramophone records. The British Flute Society and other local and national Flute Society functions in other countries are also useful in the same way; go to the meetings and ask. Having found someone 'really good', justify the lessons. (See under THE PROPER PUPIL.) The teacher can't work miracles; that's up to you.

Advanced Level: Firstly, don't look *only* for the famous player. A good flute player is not always a good teacher, though there are likely to be more *good* teachers amongst the ranks of good players. The two skills, teaching and performing, require different talents. The performer performs; the teacher has to impart the knowledge to enable the pupil to perform. Doing it, knowing how to do it, and the ability to communicate that knowledge, aren't so closely related as one might think.

There is no more reason why a great performer should be a good teacher than he should be a good mathematician, though the chances of his being a good teacher of his instrument are greater. He is, after all, conversant with the technique of the instrument; whether or not he can communicate the mysteries of his acquired knowledge is another matter.

A teacher who has had to think out every step, and who has encountered many of the basic technical flute problems, has more chance of being a better teacher, but it is by no means certain.

By far the most valuable gift a good teacher possesses is enthusiasm. Not just enthusiasm for playing, but enthusiasm for teaching. For him, the pleasure is in building up and helping others, and the enjoyment of encouraging enthusiasm. So ask around where flute players gather. Advanced players who are considering flute playing as a career should treat the finding of a proper teacher as a matter of urgency. (See AUDITIONS.)

FLUTE SCHOOLS

The widely-travelled performer would agree that there are national characteristics of flute playing in each country. Usually these are the result of the influence of one or more well-known performers in that country. Travel, records and radio are gradually blurring these differences.

The so-called French School is the most widely known. What precisely is this School? It is largely a concept of playing based on the enormous influence of Marcel Moyse (1889 – 1984), his teaching, his books and methods, and his playing. The French flute makers, too, have had their influence: Louis Lot, Bonneville, Lebret and others.

Moyse often rejected the idea that there ever was a 'school'; "If it has to have a name," he once said, "then it's called the 'play the music and not the flute' school". Two characteristics of the French School have, however, had a marked influence on world flute playing: a light, vibrant tone, and good articulation, not to mention the wide influence of French flute repertoire. That influence spread throughout the world and gave birth to a number of other schools and teaching ideals, reducing the dominance of the French School.

There are now as many schools as there are influential teachers. They all have a common goal: the mastery of the flute and the beautiful performance of music.

PRACTISING

General: Enjoyable practice of the flute comes from achievement and speedy progress. Those themselves are acquired by practising the right exercises.

Up to the age of about 16 you are growing, your muscles are flexible, fingers loose, joints supple, and your brain is well accustomed to the solving of problems. For a year or two, your body coasts along. Then, slowly, your fingers begin to work less well, technical problems are harder to overcome: your body is beginning to age.

Many young players learn the flute through pieces or solos. This is a mistake. There must be *some* music performance, at least to try out the acquired techniques, and for pure enjoyment, but it should be kept to a reasonable proportion of the available practice-time.

Music was written to provide enjoyment for both listener and performer, *and not as a technical exercise.* To acquire a good technique, or a beautiful tone, practise technique or tone exercises: they were designed for this purpose. If you have a cut on your foot, a gin and tonic may temporarily alleviate the suffering, but it won't cure the problem.

Practice-time should be divided up into four parts: tone, technique, studies (including articulation) and repertoire.

Try to practise at the same time every day. Why? Because your body behaves like a clockwork machine: everything about it is rhythmical. If that's the way the horse is going, ride it that way. Some difficult technical exercises are made more effectual by practising them at the same time each day. Why this is, isn't relevant. It just is. Try it. If you can't keep to the same time, practise at another time rather than not at all.

If you can't sleep at night, advertisers suggest you have a hot, milky, malt drink before retiring. It works, but only after a week or more. The same effect can be achieved by drinking a glass of water before going to bed, or scratching your right ear. It's the *regularity* which makes it work, not *what* you do. It's the same with practice. Regular practice doesn't usually result in constant regular improvement: sometimes it levels off for a while − or appears to − before improvement is noticed.

Tone exercises are interesting in this respect. If you haven't practised any before, the first thing you will notice is that, after a few days, your tone is worse! That's normal. Your tone isn't *really* worse, but your perception of it has become more acute: you are observing your tone at close quarters. Notes are held, and examined, for a relatively long period and defects are noticed, perhaps for the first time. A fleeting glance in the mirror doesn't reveal your acne: a close scrutiny does.

Tone exercises won't in themselves improve tone. What will is partly the human desire to *sound nice* and partly the playing of long notes, together with the observance of defects, which allows this human desire to take the upper hand. Long notes are, by their very nature, likely to effect an improvement. That means *long* notes. Looking at the clock won't help.

Technical exercises, regularly practised, improve your technique over a period of time but it is often not a regular, gradual improvement.

Any alteration of the hand position is also going to result in a temporary setback. Changing, though, does mean that your finger muscles will be properly exercised and encouraged to be independent of each other: a vital path to a good finger technique.

How to Practise Technique: Use a metronome. It's surprising how the tempo varies from day to day depending on your mood, the difficulties to be overcome, the weather, or how late you stayed up last night.

Use the most difficult fingering as much as possible. This will give more exercise for the fingers and is, in the long term, the shortest route to finger independence.

In difficult technical exercises, although the metronome provides a basic beat, *each note* should have a beat or count, in your head. This will help you gain greater accuracy and control over your fingers. Practise difficult passages slowly, of course; everyone is taught to do this. But don't *always* practise slowly, or you will not gain the experience of controlling your fingers at fast speeds. Practising passages in different rhythms helps, too, but beware that this kind of practice doesn't become an end in itself. The whole objective is to play accurately, in tune, and with a 'clean' technique. A good tone is important, too. It is surprising how a technical difficulty can demoralize you to the point where this is reflected in your tone. Try to remind yourself about this point.

No technical exercise should be practised once pain in the fingers or hand is felt. This is particularly important when re-adjusting your posture or hand position. If this should happen, practise several times a day for short periods.

The objective of technical exercises is to reach a point where your fingers allow you, unimpeded, to perform the music. The fingers need to be independent of each other; when you command a finger to move, it is irritating when its neighbour moves as well.

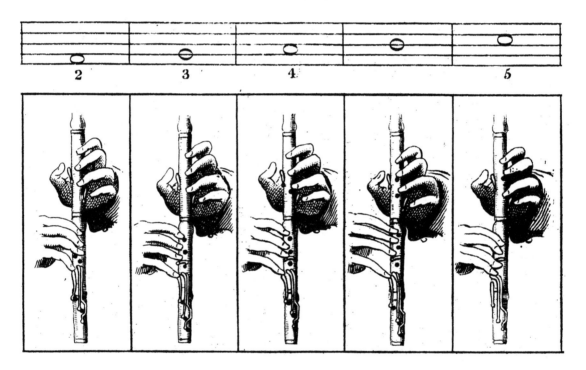

From Nicholson's *Preceptive Lessons* (1816)

The important rule is: use the *correct fingering*. If you use the wrong fingering, you cheat yourself. Here is a list of objectives:

1) Use the D sharp key when moving from D to either E or F in the low and middle registers, not *after* you've played but at the moment when E or F is played.

2) Use the third finger for F sharp. The middle finger F sharp is flat and of poor quality and should be used only for trills, or in the third octave to prevent sharpness.

3) Use the first finger of the right hand for B flat. The B flat thumb key is easy and needs no practice. The 'long' B flat is used in the keys with lots of sharps and flats, therefore get accustomed to it now.

4) Finger middle E flat correctly, that is, with the first finger of the left hand raised.★

5) Top B natural and C are played *without* the little finger on the D sharp key.

★See *Practice Book 3 – Articulation –* page 28.

6) When playing quickly from B flat to A in the first two octaves, be sure to remove the first finger of the right hand for A, assuming, of course, that you are using the 'long' B flat.

If you follow these rules, all the practice that you do should result in a 'clean' and in-tune technique.

The Muscles: There are two aspects of a fast, clean technique to be considered: a) the number of notes per second, or speed; and b) the time taken for the fingers and thumb to rise and fall from the keys. Speed alone is insufficient: to acquire a really clean technique, the fingers too must rise and fall quickly, or the fast scales which you hope to acquire will sound blurred.

Getting On With It: a) Start with the exercises in *Practice Book 2 – Technique –* page 7; when *any* misfingering or uncertainty appears, refer to, and practise, the Scale Exercises on page 14. When sufficient fluency has been gained, then, and *only* then, tackle them in the third octave. The reason for this is that you are practising finger independence and movement. These techniques are more easily acquired in the first two octaves; the third octave is more difficult (because it is played less often) and relies on a reasonably firm technique in the first two octaves. The third octave is also very tiring for the lips – and your neighbours!

b) Find a book of studies (there is a list at the back of this book) which is within your reach, and practise one study for at least a week. Don't peck at it: divide it into sections and work on each section every day.

Covering the whole compass is important to the acquisition of a clean and Proper technique; scale and finger exercises alone cannot provide the necessary movement between octaves. Some daily work in moving around the flute is necessary, or your lips become accustomed to one register only.

Tone: Be sure to have an objective in mind when playing tone exercises. In this way you will achieve greater progress than by staring out of the window. If, or when, your lips get tired, rest for a short while before continuing. Make a mental note of any interesting tone changes made whilst experimenting. Try to feel good in yourself: happy, perhaps even exhilarated. It will all add a bit more 'glow' to what you do.

Articulation: This is difficult to practise for long periods. The base of the tongue gets tired quite quickly. Try flutter tonguing – using the tip of your tongue – between bouts of practice: it will help to relax your tongue. Articulation isn't something you can tackle to the exclusion of all other problems: it needs frequent short bursts of practice. Use two music stands: on one keep the current book of studies, on the second, your articulation exercises. This way, you can switch from one to the other without wasting time.

Intonation: This has to be part of your technique, tone, and studies practice. Check all the usual flute playing 'nasties' during scales, such as sharp C sharps, flat low notes, and flat middle E and F, not to mention the particularly sharp notes in the third octave, E flat, E natural, F sharp, B natural and C. Fingerings can be found in *Practice Book 6* to help the intonation problems of the third octave.

Studies: How would *you* set about writing a book of studies? You will need one in every key, so that makes 24. Why every key? It's crazy to limit yourself to playing pieces only in G or F major. Some keys are especially powerful and dramatic in grand melodies, such as A flat major. Imagine that you've just heard a piece on the radio and then you order it at your local music shop only to find it is in F sharp minor, a key with which you are unfamiliar. You would be unable to play it. A Proper flute player will be familiar with every key. Studies reflect the difficulties likely to be encountered in pieces. So, a book of studies should have one in every key.

Next, each study should bring to the player's notice certain technical problems, such as a variety of articulation, difficult combinations of notes, leaps from one octave to another, accidentals for reading practice, and so on. What else? Most important of all, studies should be *musical*. They should be sufficiently musically interesting, and challenging, to be satisfying. Sometimes they are not. A list of recommended studies will be found at the back of this book.

Having acquired a suitable book, now to work. Mark the passages which you find difficult and practise these every day. The study was probably designed to be medicinal with a bit of sugar-coating, in order to make it more palatable: it's the medicinal bit you should be getting on with. Most often, the first few lines are practised more than the middle section. The next day, *start* at the middle section.

Practise what you can't do. Whatever problems you encounter you can be sure that everyone before you has had the same difficulty. That may be some comfort.

Articulation studies should be practised together with legato studies. Rapid tonguing, in particular, *is* tiring and it is wisest to practise two studies in the same day, a legato study which is currently being worked on and a long-term articulation study which is practised in short bursts between longer sessions on the legato study.

In general, a study should be practised for no more than two or three weeks, or until you come to a full stop with it. It's like a piece of gymnastic apparatus: a point is arrived at where you have extracted all you can within your ability. Any further work on it becomes an obsession with completion of the entire study for completion's sake. This isn't necessary: move on to the next one. Studies are written for exercise. Ideally, it is better to be able to *play* the whole study but that shouldn't be an end in itself. If you've improved in the course of practising it, then that's enough; go back to it in a year or so.

It is important that musicality and expression should be a large part of practising studies. It is a pointless pursuit to practise a passage purely to learn the notes and then add the expression later. Kissing can't be learned by acting out the motions and adding the expression later. Flute playing – and cooking – can't either. All the ingredients should be present. The practice of being expressive is part of practice. Your powers of expression need to develop and you can only achieve this by making expression a part of your daily practice.

Interval Studies: The objective here is to minimize the lip and jaw movements necessary to obtain the notes in a passage in which the notes leap around. This must first be practised slowly. Read the section 'Flexibility' on page 27 of *Practice Book 1 – Tone*, then practise the first exercise, attempting to make each note beautiful.

We have a tendency to play such an exercise with a lip, jaw and airstream combination common to all the notes. In other words, we find an embouchure in which all the notes can be produced easily, but not necessarily with a beautiful tone. To begin with, practise each of the first four notes, noting the tiny movements which have to be made in order to play *each* note with a beautiful tone. *It's the supple muscular change between notes which is the whole purpose of this section, 'Flexibility'.*

Do it slowly at first. These exercises are tiring for the lips and should be practised in the beginning for a short time only. Increase the time spent on them as your lips become stronger. You will observe that the movement of the lips diminishes, the longer the exercises are practised.

Scales: Easily the most important part of acquiring technical fluency. Scales must cover all the compass that you know – if you aren't yet familiar with the top end of the third octave, then practise the Daily Exercises in the third octave, adding one extra top note every two weeks or so. The Proper flute player plays scales expressively.

The scales and arpeggios set out in *Practice Book 5* are not only an ideal to aim at, they are there for regular daily practice, even if you can already play them.

> The foregoing SCALES, are, in the Author's opinion, the best and most de-sirable Studies either in this or any other work which it has fallen to his lot to peruse, and the acquirement of them he considers most indispensably necessary to every per-former desirous of excelling on the Flute.
>
> They should be practised quite slow at first, gradually increasing the Time, on each repetition, until they can be played with equal rapidity, smoothness, and precision.
>
> It will be found exceedingly difficult to accomplish this, but a well—directed practice will effect every thing, and the time thus spent in the acquirement of the Scales, will be more than amply repaid by giving the student that perfect freedom and command of his Instrument, in all the Keys, which it is impossible to get by any other mode of practice.
>
> The advantages, indeed, to every pupil who will take the trouble of making himself master of the Scales, are incalculable; and although their continued prac-tice may (and most likely *will*) be considered irksome and uninteresting, — yet let it always be recollected, that as "There is no Royal Road to Learning," neither is good Flute Playing to be acquired without study and application; — that there is, perhaps, no pleasure without its concomitant pain; — and that "He who would eat Fruit, must first climb the Tree to get it."

From Nicholson's *Preceptive Lessons* (1816)

A Daily Practice Schedule: Some rules first. Rules, because they will help you become better quicker, thereby allowing you to spend more time on the beach, or more time on what else amuses you besides the flute.

a) Whatever time you have to practise, make it *really* effective.

b) If you don't know why you are practising an exercise, then stop. You should have an *objective*, apart from doing it because it's there.

c) If you hesitate frequently while practising then cut down on the hesitations. Try to maintain a continuous stream of sound.

d) Practise at the same time each day, if possible.

e) Avoid practising difficult technical exercises or tone exercises continuously for more than forty minutes; play a different exercise and go back to the first exercise later in the day.

Here are some suggested schedules depending on the time available:
40 minutes a day 15 minutes on tone exercises; 10 minutes on finger exercises; 15 minutes on a study. At weekends and once during the week, get to grips with some pieces.

1 hour a day As above but extend the practice of studies to 20 minutes; the remainder to be spent on pieces.

2 hours a day 20 minutes on tone exercises; the more serious player should practise 20 minutes on finger exercises (*Practice Books 2* or *6*); 30 minutes on studies. Later in the day, another 20 minutes on finger exercises; the remainder of the time to be spent on special problems (articulation, intonation, etc.) and pieces.

3 or 4 hours a day 1 hour on tone, including warming up, tone colour exercises, melodies, expressive scales and arpeggios (*Practice Book 5*); 1 hour on technique, including finger exercises and scales; 1 hour on studies, including articulation; the remainder of the time to be spent on special problems, repertoire pieces and orchestral excerpts.

These are rough guides only. Try to get into the *habit* of daily practice and make it as effective as you can. The Proper flute player makes his practice really effective so that he can spend more time at the beach.

THE BASIC ELEMENTS OF TECHNIQUE

Posture: This is the first building block of a good player. It's also common sense.

Proper flute playing at the highest level requires that a number of elements be right. A weakness in any one reduces the chances of attaining excellence. Even in advanced performers the teacher has to refer occasionally to the basic elements of posture, standing correctly, the head-body-flute relationship, and the hand positions.

There isn't a photo one can copy; there is no fixed position we must all adopt. Bodies, heads, arms and hands differ, but the principles remain the same. An incorrect head-body-flute relationship can cause horrid problems as the player becomes more advanced, such as a bleating vibrato, a tight throat, pains in the back or neck, a poor tone, etc. The longer a poor position is maintained, the harder it will be to correct all the spin-offs from this bad position. The solution is, *correct it now.*

To function properly, the hands and body should be encouraged to operate from a position of relaxation.

Head-Body-Flute Relationship: Lean with your back against a wall or door, flute in hand, with head, body and feet all facing directly to the front. *Without moving your head,* bring the flute to your mouth.

The flute is played sideways?

Wrong.

The flute is played almost to the front of your body.

Playing the flute sideways, as in a marching band,

POSTURE

creates some of the worst problems encountered in flute playing, such as a bleating vibrato, a tight throat (and therefore, blowing problems), poor articulation, not to mention backache, arm ache and neck ache, and, in consequence, for your audience, earache.

Look at diagrams 1 and 2.

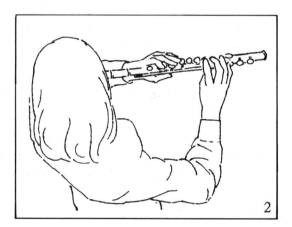

These diagrams are from the *Beginner's Practice Book* (Novello).

Once again, with your back to a wall, hold the flute in front of you like an oboe, recorder or clarinet. Without moving your shoulders, turn your head to your left. Not just your eyeballs, your head as well. *Don't turn your head too far:* just look at your left elbow. Now, without moving your head, bring the flute to your mouth.

The flute is played away from the front of your body. Fine, so far. The problems start when you approach a music stand.

When you are next talking to someone in the street, slowly move around them, in a circle. *They* will move too, in order to face you. When we talk to people, we are more comfortable when we are directly facing them with our heads and bodies than if we are looking at them with our heads turned to the right or left.

The music stand is like a person: it's offering information, or communicating to us. Therefore, we naturally face the music stand both with our faces and our feet. OK so far? The trouble starts when the flute is brought up to the playing position: the body has to be twisted in order to see the music.

Walk to the music stand; turn your body about 45° to your right (feet as well), turn your head to your left to face the stand. Check that your shoulders and elbows are relaxed, and there you are.

Orchestral seating, too, needs some alteration or adjustment. The chair needs to be turned *away* from the oboes, and the stand placed so as to be in line with the new head position and the conductor.

Changing your posture won't get rid of all your problems straight away. As stated before, unlearning and re-learning is a long job, during the course of which your body, unused to these changes, will find it tiring. It may cause backache and neck ache for a while whilst the change is taking place. At worst, it will take a week or two to go.

But, to be a Proper flute player, it has to be done.

The Right Hand: Let your right hand go limp. Look at it. The fingers are curved, the thumb is *sideways-on* to the index or first finger. Don't turn the thumb sideways as if *gripping* the flute. Don't then straighten the little ('pinky') finger to a point where it is used curved upwards.

Ask someone to hold your thumb and little 'pinky' finger in *that* position and then try moving the third finger − the one next to the little finger. It can only be moved by *overcoming the tension caused by the unnatural position of the thumb and little finger.* Worse news yet. Technical exercises designed to acquire finger independence become exercises in working *against your own tension;* a tension created in the first place by you! *You are working against yourself.*

Look at diagram 3.

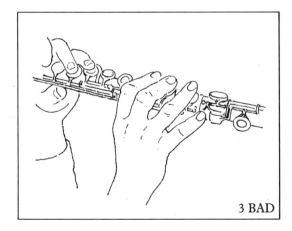

3 BAD

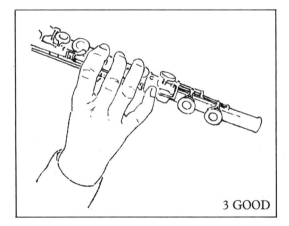

3 GOOD

To change isn't easy. An exaggeratedly correct hand position has to be adopted: turn the wrist towards the foot end of the flute whilst pivoting on the side of the thumb, until the little finger is operating on its side. After a week or two, the hand can gradually relax into a more natural position. Even then, constant vigilance will be required to maintain the new position. See the exercises in *Practice Book 2 – Technique*. (Better than seeing them, practise them!) It needs a lot of self-discipline. Like many corrective procedures it won't make everything better immediately; observation of faulty foundations won't stop the building falling down. Only curing the fault will do that, and even then the building, if it is to become higher, will increasingly rely on all the other building blocks of technique. Weaknesses in basics will show up eventually. The higher you go, or the more advanced you become, the more wobbly will be the structure. *PUT IT RIGHT NOW,* if you wish to be a Proper flute player.

The Left Hand: This one isn't so difficult to correct. The most common problems are, again, a straight little 'pinky' finger and third (ring) finger, and the elbow raised sometimes even to shoulder level. Both can be put right at the same time.

Look at diagram 4.

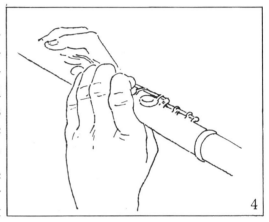

Firstly the elbow. Why raise it? The fashion for raising the elbow probably arose because many players – and therefore, teachers – were formerly in military bands. Piccolo parts can only be read when the left wrist is raised so that the lyre and its strap, which holds the music, are in line with the eyeball. Great for marching; lousy for flute playing.

This military posture leads to a support of the flute involving a lot of side pressure of the first finger to prevent the flute slipping down your chin. It doesn't need that sort of pressure. To correct it, allow the elbow to drop; at the same time, move the index finger joint (basal joint) underneath the flute, and a little closer towards the G sharp key. The thumb should be higher, and straight. The fingers should now be curved – especially the third finger and little finger – and the flute supported from *below.*

The advantages of this posture are that the flute is prevented from slipping during hot weather or as a result of nerves; the flute has adequate support; and lastly, the fingers are operating from a relaxed position. Well, almost. It has one disadvantage: the first, index, finger is slightly cramped because of the increased sharp angle at which it has to operate but this is only a *minor* disadvantage.★

This new position will allow the fingers to operate correctly but will require some determination to put right, and frequent observations. Whatever headjoint position is adopted, the mechanism on which the fingers are placed should be level: that is, turned neither in nor out. If the flute is turned in, your fingers have to *hold* the flute and will be less able to do their technical job properly.

Proper support from the left hand will obviate the need for sticky paper on the lip-plate.

★Flute players and makers have encouraged this Proper arm position by making offset G flutes. In any case, they are mechanically more reliable. Boehm was concerned about the support from below and consequently devised his 'crutch', a gadget in the shape of the letter 'T' which is screwed to the underside of the flute and allows the flute to rest on the joint between first finger and thumb. A nice idea, but it seriously weakens the action of the thumb and never caught on, though it's often found on the heavier alto and bass flutes of today.

TONE

The flute was designed to be played with a beautiful tone; the cutting of the mouth-hole, its shape, the lip-plate, the taper of the headjoint, are all contributory factors. *It is quite difficult to play the flute with a bad tone.*

> Several anonymous communications having reached the Author, expressing a wish that he would explain the precise position of the Lips, Embouchure, &c: in order to produce that peculiar quality of Tone for which the best Flute Players are so much ad_mired,_he begs to refer such correspondents to his Instruction Book already before the public, where they will find this subject clearly and distinctly treated.   Convinced, however, how very inferior all written precepts are to oral instruction, in so nice a matter,_ and willing as far as possible to be serviceable to those Amateurs who may follow the course of practice pointed out in these PRECEPTIVE LESSONS, he will have much pleasure in giv_ing a Lesson *gratis* on the formation of the Embouchure &c, to all who may possess the Work when complete; and by One Lesson on this subject he feels assured that a Pupil will derive more benefit than if he were at the trouble to peruse a whole Volume.

From Nicholson's *Preceptive Lessons* (1816)

Embouchures: Every teacher has his favourite theory about mouth shapes and the correct 'faces' to pull. Some say smile; others say pull down the sides of the mouth using the lower lip like a stationary cushion, or suggest blowing in a way which least alters the natural position of the mouth. Others again encourage the puffing out of the cheeks.

All may be right in certain circumstances. I don't believe that there is one *right* way. Mr A is an international star: copying him may not be the answer for Mr B, a student of the flute. B is a different person: he may be successful in imitating A, but he would never really know the alternatives because *he has never tried them.*

The only real test of success is *if it sounds good*; no matter whether the embouchure is a relaxed one, a Suzumi one, or any other totalitarian concept of blowing.

In the diagram of the facial muscles (see below), notice that there is a preponderance of 'smiling' muscles (muscles can only pull − they can't push). The smiling embouchure can cause an overtight and overworked bottom lip and can result in embouchure problems.

'Relaxed' is a fraught word: relax this, relax that. What is meant is that the muscles must be controlled *but not rigid.* They must be capable of movement in order to deal with tone colour, nuance, octaves, etc. There cannot be a totally relaxed embouchure, or there would be *no tone. To relax is to collapse.* Moyse sums it up in the word 'supple'.

Anyone who claims success in teaching a particular 'face' also hides the inevitable failures who are themselves the result of being unable to pull that particular face *and* make a beautiful sound. Failures never become famous.

We should be guided by what *sounds* right, not only by what looks right.

Don't regard tone as a major obstacle. It isn't. The Proper understanding of what goes on in relation to the mouth and lip-plate combined, is very important to success. The Proper understanding of what goes on in relation to the mouth and lip-plate combined, is very important to success.

No, that's not a printer's error. The same sentence has been repeated.

What follows is a study of the factors involved, an understanding of which may save hours of fruitless practice!

1) The shape of the blow-hole in the lips; that's a question of some simple experiments and time spent training the muscles.

2) The amount the blow-hole is uncovered; this is *directly* proportional to the size and projection of the tone, and to the overall intonation.

3) The direction of the air; this must be discovered by experimental practice.

4) The size of the cavities in the mouth, nose and throat; you will have to experiment.

5) The quality of your headjoint and your flute; a question of your wallet, and good professional advice.

Put away any photographs, drawings or record sleeves of flute players whose 'face' you have been trying to imitate. That is a waste of time. You are *you*; no one else. The external appearance of a person's face will give little indication of what is happening inside the mouth and on the inside of the lips, which is where it's all at. You must use what *you* have to obtain the best result. To imitate a 'face' slavishly is no more useful in flute playing that copying a hairstyle, or growing a beard and acquiring an Irish accent.

Your Face: The first factor is the shape of the hole in the lips. Some teachers have a tendency to direct their pupils to imitate themselves. Sometimes it can work. Often it only works to a limited degree, and perhaps not at all. "Do what I do and you will then be as successful as me." This is a dangerous statement.

The hole between your lips that you blow through on first taking up the flute may be naturally perfect or it may not. It depends, to some extent, on the amount of use the facial muscles have had, particularly around the mouth, in everyday living. An animated face indicates frequent use of a lot of muscle. The muscles around, and attached to, your mouth look like this:

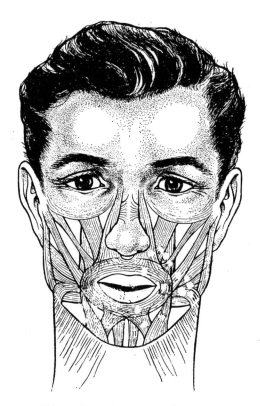

SCHEME OF MUSCULATURE OF EMBOUCHURE

It is not necessary to study the diagram in great detail. It's enough to note that there are more *separate* muscles attached to this organ than anywhere else in the human body. Our job is to adapt them for flute playing. Some muscles will be fairly passive because of lack of regular use. Whether or not they can all be persuaded to work for you in a short time is a matter of chance. For some people it will be easy, for others more difficult.

The Amount to Uncover: If the first face you made on blowing the flute sounded good, then there is a beginning. Half the job has already been done for you by good headjoint design. The other half is you.

What has the flute maker designed for you?

Firstly the scale, that is, the hole positions, each of which determines the pitch of the various notes. The headpiece was designed so that the wall against which you are going to blow, often called the strike wall, is set at an angle in relation to your lower lip to achieve the best result from the airstream directed at it.

Secondly, the lip-plate hole has to be uncovered by a certain amount or the scale which the flute plays will either be expanded or contracted. That's to say, there will be more, or less, than one octave between low C and the first finger C, depending on the amount of covering. *This is a very important point.* Do read it again.

Thirdly, the amount by which the lip-plate hole is uncovered *is directly proportional to the size of the sound and therefore its projection.* Covering too much will result in a smaller tone; uncovering too much, in a windy, unfocused tone.

Getting any one of these three factors right will usually *put the other two right at the same time.*

Air Direction: When the correct amount of uncovering of the lip-plate hole is achieved (instructions for which will follow), the airstream needs to be directed at the right angle. Some people with tone problems blow through too small a hole between their lips, or cover the hole too much and direct the airstream too high. This way of playing will result in a thin and reedy tone.

*Drawing by Maurice Porter. Reproduced from "Dental Problems In Wind Instrument Playing" by permission of British Dental Journal

Others blow through too large a hole and uncover the blow-hole too much. This way of blowing can sound windy and unfocused.

For most people, the edge of the embouchure hole is best placed at the edge of the red part of the lip, that is if you have an average sized lower lip. If the lip-plate is too high on the lip, it will be difficult to focus the tone.

Freedom of Choice: When we begin to play the flute, the type of tone we produce is most likely the result of the natural formation of our mouths and throats. This means that we haven't given ourselves a truly free choice. The beginner is happy to have produced a nice tone. The experiments and exercises which follow are designed to encourage you to make two extremes of tone colour and to enable you subsequently to fill in the colours between these extremes. For the sake of clarity I've called the two colours yellow and purple.

You, the reader, may not want to play the flute with a wide range of tone colours. OK, but that's not the point of these exercises. The artist may be perfectly happy to draw in black using white paper. If you wish to make only one kind of sound, then the choice of colour will be yours. The exercises will help you to experiment with a whole palette of colours out of which you will be *free to choose* one, or more, of the colours, in order to paint your musical picture.

Even if your present flute tone is entirely to your satisfaction, these exercises will allow you the *choice* of change. If you were going out to buy a sweater, it would be wisest to go to a shop with the widest choice of styles and colours.

Let's summarize what has been learnt so far and list the desirable attributes for a beautiful tone:

1) It needs a centre core, or what is often called 'focus'.

2) It needs to project; modern day orchestral playing often calls for strength and 'carrying quality'.

3) It should be in tune.

4) The player needs to be able to produce different colours in order to sound interesting and to meet the needs of the composer.

SOME TONE EXPERIMENTS

This is a series of experiments, of which each one is a possible ingredient in your recipe to achieve the sound of your choice.

Projection: *The lowest sound frequencies travel the greatest distances.* Their amplitude is directly related to the 'size of tone' and projection even though the higher frequencies sound louder to the player. Rolling the headjoint out − in other words, uncovering the embouchure hole − will diminish the volume of the few upper partials the flute possesses, and increase the strength of the fundamental, or lowest harmonic; what we call the lowest note. It follows that tone exercises have to be based on a recipe in which the fundamental is as large as possible, relative to the upper harmonics. (If you are frowning when reading this, then look at *Practice Book 4 − Intonation* − the first part.)

If your tone is small; if you want more variety; if you are usually sharp, especially in the third octave, and flat in the low octave; then *turn out, pull the headjoint out,* and *blow down.* Three simple rules. Begin your experiments by playing low G.

Turning out will achieve immediate loudness and will allow, in time, more variety and will certainly increase the size of the tone. *But,* it may not sound nice; therefore, blow downwards. DON'T put your head down to do this, or the embouchure hole will be re-covered. The bottom lip is the coverer; to blow down, the top lip needs to project more and the chin needs to be moved back.

So, when you try this your reactions may be a) it sounds windy and fuzzy; b) the tone is rather wild; c) you can't play softly; and d) you use more air.

The answer is that to sound bigger needs a drastic change; in time, the quality will re-appear; there will be less and less air escaping; and finally you will, after practice, be able to play softly and *in tune* again.

By turning the headjoint in and covering the embouchure hole too much, a false tone is produced, which is a recipe containing strong upper partials and little fundamental. We say that the sound is buzzy. What is strange is that this tone quality sounds loud to the player but *small and directional* to the listener; a sort of 'keyhole' effect. When some exercises have been practised with the embouchure hole more uncovered, the directional buzziness becomes less marked and, if the airstream is also lowered, the tone appears to come from a general area, rather than from a fixed point. The player is often unaware of this. You need a good teacher or another player or, at least, another pair of sensitive ears to help check what's happening.

Having uncovered more of the embouchure hole, you will be sharp. So *pull out the headjoint*. Within reason, and without losing control of the tone, the more you pull out, the better. The amount of air available in the tube to vibrate is increased by another small, but noticeable amount. Good, eh?

The first experiment is on low G: try parting your lips more than usual, making a slightly wider gap between the front teeth. Don't raise the direction of the air. If this larger hole makes a difference, remember how it feels, and use it when trying to sound hollow and large. It may open up the sides of the hole through your lips and increase the amount of air escaping; this can be controlled in time. The point is, does it improve your tone?

The second experiment: try *slowly* changing the cavities in your mouth and throat. These cavities have much more effect on your tone than you may realize. You do this by partially yawning – not too much, as it causes tension – and moving your tongue around. Try this on one note only. Remember to make a mental note of any improvement or change.

It is not true that the larger you can make the mouth and throat cavities, the bigger the tone, though players who are physically bigger have less difficulty in acquiring a large tone. Each note requires a different *volume of air in the mouth*, and throat, the same as the flute itself. Only by experiment can this be realized.

The third experiment: this one is related to, but not always the same as, the second experiment. Play a long, low G, and every second, change the shape in your mouth as in saying A-E-I-O-U. Observe any changes in the tone quality. Make a mental note of any interesting sounds.

If you've made some observations, now use them to assist you to find the colours in the flute tone.

The Low Register – A Yellow Tone: Practise the *Aquarium* tune⋆ and use the three experiments above to help you find a really hollow, beautiful, big but *buzzless* tone. A yellow colour. Be expressive. You will be using up far more air than before. That problem will be dealt with at the end of this section. Avoid tension or rigidity in your lips. Experiment with the air *direction*.

Perhaps the lowest note of the exercise, the whole note or minim, hasn't got the same big open quality? Then go down in stages using bars 5, 6 and 7, to practise getting down to the lowest note. No wasps yet, please.

This *Aquarium* exercise, and the previous experiments, should occupy almost your entire practice time for a week or more. Give up pieces, studies, scales, orchestral playing and busking. You *can* do some finger exercises using the new tone.

How to Use Less Air: Now, spend another week or ten days on the next stage, which is: play the same exercises above, but, without any loss of volume and still observing the crescendos marked, try to use *half as much air*. It will be an exercise for your lips to find the most economical

⋆See *Practice Book 1 – Tone –* page 9.

use of the air supply. Try to keep the same big sound. This can take time and should become part of your practice. The lip muscles have to find the way of producing a good yellow tone with less air.

Properly practise these exercises first, before going on to the next section.

A Purple Tone: The next stage is to try to produce a totally different colour from the open, gentle, hollow *Aquarium* tone. The Ravel tune on page 10 in *Practice Book 1 – Tone* is ideal for this.

The object is to make the same *sound* as in *Aquarium* but to *add* harmonics to it. If you were to turn the flute in, or cover more, it would certainly add harmonics but, at the same time, *it would diminish the fundamental,* with a resulting loss of projection, and the notes will be flat. Your listeners will hear a thin, buzzy sound.

The rich, strong colour has to be practised by building on top of what has already been learned in the *Aquarium* tune. *The hollow 'yellow' fundamental tone is the basis on which to add harmonics to produce a purple sound.*

That last statement should be clearly understood. It's better to play *Aquarium* with this purple colour first, partly because you will already be familiar with the tune, and partly to check on any change of pitch. The pitch must be the same as in the yellow colour or the change will indicate that the blow-hole has been covered more. Don't do that. Use the centre of your lips to hold the airstream and direct it downward.

Each day from now on, practise making the two sounds as *different* as possible: yellow and purple, but at the same dynamic level. (Not easy!) Later, it will be possible to fill in the colours between the two extremes. At this stage, aim for the widest possible difference of colour.

The *Aquarium* tone will be quieter; practise it louder, *without* changing the colour. That *is* difficult, but *yellow isn't a weak colour, it's simply yellow.*

At this point, if you are in doubt about your ability to play loudly and softly in tune, read the section in this book called 'Playing Loudly and Softly in the First Two Octaves'.

The Second Octave: The next stage is to spread those two colours into the middle and upper registers. (See the exercises and explanation on pages 17 and 18 of *Practice Book 1 – Tone.)* Spreading the tone, of whichever colour, to the middle octave can be difficult for a while. The trick is *don't raise the airstream to go up.* It's tempting because you may have done this for years. Raising the airstream by a *tiny amount* is necessary to maintain the correct pitch; but for the moment, don't. If you do raise the airstream, the colour is lost. Raising the air direction may produce quite a pretty sound but it won't be the *same* sound as in the lower register. *The second octave must have,* as nearly as possible, *the same colour as the first octave.*

Practise the octaves firstly on page 13 of *Practice Book 1,* and when you have overcome the habit of raising the airstream, then practise the exercises on page 17.

If the instructions so far have been followed, the middle E on page 17 will often crack. Good. It means that you are using a tone which is very close to the point where the note is likely to drop into the low octave. Learning just *where* that point is, is the whole objective of the first few days of practice. Raising the airstream and, therefore, changing the colour, *loses* the whole object of the exercise. You would be better off at the beach. The E will crack most often when using the purple sound.

Soon, the tone will crack less and less often on middle E. The E will have the sonority of your low register. More important still, *the colour of the middle octave will very nearly match the colour of the low register.*

These pages of exercises in *Practice Book 1* should be worked at for some time. Only when the middle E is mastered is it time to go on to the Tone Colour exercises on page 24. These exercises, in effect, will serve to cement the two octaves together. Eventually, the same process is used to gain a foothold – or a mouth hold – on the high register (see page 18 of *Practice Book 1).*

20

The Upper Register: Raising the airstream changes the tone; the pitch also rises. Don't turn the headjoint in to go into the third octave. *Don't try*, at this stage, to play softly.

Now go on to pages 20 and 21 of *Practice Book 1*: spend plenty of time on them and also on pages 34, 35 and 36.

Now turn to the back of *Practice Book 4 – Intonation* and practise the 24 studies. Put in louds and softs wherever you like, but *exaggerate* them. (Without any *real* louds or softs, a player *could* resort to choreography.)*

Playing Loudly and Softly in the First Two Octaves: A common ailment amongst flute players is a lack of contrast in loud and soft playing. Many young players seem to have no understanding of the principles involved. They are simple: to play softly, use less air; this makes the note go flat. To prevent it going flat, the blow-hole needs to be uncovered. Combine the two, and you have it. But how?

By pushing the jaw forward the blow-hole is uncovered.** To make a really soft sound it needs uncovering more. So you may have to use your head *and* change the air direction as well. By tilting your head back slightly the hole will be more uncovered and thus prevent the note becoming flat. Before attempting this, it is essential to get some degree of mobility, first with the jaw and lips, and, if this is insufficient, the head as well. The exercise on page 34 in *Practice Book 1* should first be practised.

Holding your flute in the playing position, nod your head up and down as if indicating 'yes'. Don't move your flute deliberately, but let it *pivot* on the first finger and thumb of your left hand. Now blow whilst doing this. You should be able to vary the pitch at least a whole tone, maybe even as much as a minor or a major third.

This mobility exercise is most important, too, for the discovery of where you are in directing the airstream, and will be of great assistance in searching for the colours and the focus of your tone. In making the swoops from C natural down to A, or as low as you can, and back again, there is another important point which should be observed. The 'best' tone is when the blow-hole is opened out *one more notch* than it *seems* best to you. That may appear to be odd. Your extra 'ears', your friend, will tell you that even when *you* think it sounds best, focused, alive, big, etc, your friend, who should be 20 feet or more away, will confirm that it sounds *bigger and warmer* when the embouchure hole is opened out a notch, or when you raise your head by a small amount.

That leads us to the conclusion that we do not hear ourselves as others hear us. We hear the flute from a distance of five or six inches, but our audiences are not on our shoulders. How *do* we know when it sounds best? By opening out one more notch than we *think* we should.

Now on to Note Endings:*** they should be practised as indicated but ensuring that the diminuendo reaches a *fine needle point* at its softest. Keep the colour through the diminuendo. With your jaw back and your head in the lower position, blow loudly, make a diminuendo, and, at the same time move your jaw forward and, if necessary, tilt your head back as well. The note will stay fairly well in tune, albeit a bit wobbly, but it will *diminuendo*. Hooray!

This technique needs plenty of practice and discipline.

Don't attempt page 36 until you can make needle point diminuendos with some skill, and in tune. Some nice melodies will help at this stage.

*See 'Choreography' later in this book.

**Yes, there does seem to be a conflict here: raising the airstream to prevent a note becoming flat will change the colour. It isn't possible to keep the colour *perfectly constant* when playing loudly and softly. Much can be achieved by intelligent practice.

***See page 35 of *Practice Book 1*.

The sections 'Mobility', 'Note Endings and Nuances', and 'Intonation' are essential for any kind of phrasing, louds and softs, and pitch control.

If you can't do this, you will never play music. That sounds tough, but the flute is quite a boring instrument. A whole flute recital can be dull. It's the *music* which makes it more bearable. To play a piece with little or no dynamic contrast − and I don't mean slight changes, I mean big ones! − is pointless. A computer can do it better. There has to be more to flute playing than the mere performance of the right notes in the right place.

If you can't play loudly and softly, you *can*, of course, resort to some elbow-waving and knee-bending choreography. It's your choice.

Intonation: This has been dealt with in some detail in the various *Practice Books* (*Book 1* page 37, *Book 4*, and *Book 6* pages 27, 28 and 35). The most common cause of bad intonation is the airstream being aimed too high at the blow-hole and/or the hole being too covered or uncovered. (This has been outlined in the previous section in this book, 'Playing Loudly and Softly in the First Two Octaves'.) It all appears to stem from our first lessons as a beginner. We are anxious to learn more notes. We reach middle D; then we try middle E; it drops down an octave. Is there some key to be opened for the second octave? No. How then? Raise the airstream, or push the jaw forward or blow harder, we are told. That achieves the desired result, but it also makes the second octave sharper than the first. Quelle horreur!

Later, into the third octave, the same problem is encountered and the same solution offered. The third octave, therefore, will become *even sharper* than the second. In time the player realizes that the second, and the most used octave, is sharp, so he pulls out. The result, then, is a flat first octave, an in-tune second octave, and a sharp third octave. *And that is a carbon copy of most flute players.*

It's not wrong to suggest raising the airstream to get the second octave *for a beginner*, as inability to get the second octave causes anxiety at that stage, and is better satisfied. But it has to be unlearned later; no great problem. It's all in the previous section in this book and in *Practice Book 1* pages 13 and 18 where it says 'don't raise the airstream too high'. In fact, it would be better not to raise the airstream at all. Sceptical? Then check with a tuning meter. The proof is in the swinging needle. A tuning meter is an expensive toy but has a limited use. Try to borrow one. Use it for observation, not correction; that's a job for your ear.
All that is achieved in tone production must be related to intonation.

Playing Softly in the Third Octave: The fingering of the third octave, from upper D to the top, is based on the third and fourth harmonics of the first octave. To produce these notes requires an airspeed three or four times faster than in the low register. To increase the airspeed, we can blow harder, or reduce the aperture in our lips, which causes less air to travel at a faster speed. A lack of confidence − and a resulting reduction in the force of the airstream − usually results in the note dropping to a lower harmonic − this most often occurs on E natural (on a flute without a split E) and F sharp.

To gain confidence and to avoid turning the flute in so as to 'squeeze' out the note, it is necessary to experiment: play top F but raise the airstream so that it *misses* the hole (raise it until you are blowing up your nose, if you like!). As you do this, use an airspeed which is *faster* than would normally be required for F. (Think of top B natural for example and use the airspeed as for *this* note.)

There should be no sound. The airstream is missing the hole. Slowly lower the ribbon of air until it *just touches* the edge of the blow-hole. *Don't* reduce the air speed. You may need several attempts at this. The result, after several tries, should be a *very* soft top F. And, it may be sharp! Repeat the experiment now on F sharp and so on, to top B or C.
This experiment can tell us that covering the hole and trying to squeeze air through it results in a *flat* F − or a raspberry!
In *Practice Book 1 − Tone −* page 23, practise exercise 1A, continuing the scale to top B or C. Finally, practise exercise 5 on page 21 as softly as you can manage. You will discover how to lower the airstream in order to play in tune.

Further Tone Practice: After your weeks of experiments, you will now need a book of tunes to try out your different colours. Marcel Moyse compiled just such a book called *Tone Development Through Interpretation* (MCA). If this doesn't appeal, then there are plenty of good tunes in the nineteenth-century repertoire and in the French School composers such as Hüe, Gaubert, Taffanel, Fauré, Debussy, Honneger, Satie, and many others. The slow sections of these and other works will enable you to practise using your tone colours whilst moving from one octave to another.

Fast pieces are really just slow pieces speeded up. Well, they are as far as tone control is concerned. There is, however, a problem to be encountered of which you should be aware: *the faster the music moves around, the more difficult it is to keep a good projecting tone.* The reason for this is that we all have a tendency to turn the flute head in when playing quickly, especially when interval leaps appear; even more so when the leaps are of an octave or more. We turn the flute head inwards because leaps are *easier to play when the mouth-hole is more covered.* (See 'Nineteenth-Century Style'.)

Regular practice of studies containing leaps should be part of your practice schedule but watch out or your tone will become smaller.

Articulation: There is little to add to the relevant sections of the *Practice Book* series, save to say that good articulation will take time. Therefore, as stated before, don't set out to practise articulation as a sole project. Alternate between legato studies and scales, and ones using various articulations.

The most important points to watch are:

a) Tongue forward. That is, tongue against or between the front teeth. Moving the tongue further back delays the start of the note.

b) The lips should be still. Any unnecessary movement should be avoided. Use a mirror to check.

c) The objective for fast, clean tonguing is to keep the action in the front of the tongue; if the base of the tongue moves unduly, it will interfere with the airstream causing untidiness and ugly articulation.

d) Move the tongue quickly, neatly and *as little as possible.*

To acquire a neat, clear and fast articulation will take time, for most people many months. The base of the tongue usually moves unnecessarily in articulating; to confine the movement to the front of the tongue only, so that the back of the tongue is fairly still, requires patience.

A more thorough explanation can be found in *Practice Book 6* on page 26. Since that volume was written, the author has been shown a film on the subject of articulation made by Dr Jochen Gärtner of West Germany. The film shows sideways-on X-rays of some eminent French and German players and students demonstrating a variety of articulations. The combination of the soundtrack and the film substantiates all the points enumerated above; the French players were by far the best for neat, clean articulation.

We are indebted to Dr Gärtner for his work in this field and for proving conclusively what was previously known only from personal experience.

AUDITIONS

At any kind of audition, whether for school, college, university or an orchestral audition, the onus is on the applicant to prove his worth. Some players audition in the belief that it's up to the interviewer to find out what the candidate can and can't do. Not so. The organization concerned advertises, and you, the candidate, step forward to say "I'm the very person you are looking for". The organization writes back to say "Thanks for your application, please come at 11.30 on Wednesday morning and prove it".

The rest is up to you.

Some General Advice – Dress: Look the part. An applicant who appears with purple hair, a shirt unbuttoned to the waist and wearing metal-studded jacket, jeans and jogging pumps, doesn't look the part. Looking 'different' in itself is no crime, and does not affect the ability of the applicant, but does *decrease his credibility in the eyes of the audition panel.*

The panel may hold the belief, rightly or wrongly, that an applicant who wears razor blades, freaky hair and curious clothing, is disfiguring himself, and this may be an outward sign of a warped personality. And it is personality which may eventually decide the outcome when there are several good candidates to choose from.

On the other hand, the panel may believe that such clothing is a sign of individuality and independence, important attributes for students of the performing arts.

The answer is to play a role: *look* like the candidate who is most likely to be acceptable in the eyes of the panel. You are not in the business of educating

CURIOUS CLOTHING

them regarding modern dress or behaviour; you want to be offered a place. Therefore, fit in.

The reverse, too, can be offputting: a lady applicant who is over-made-up or over-dressed can, in the panel's eyes, look like someone who is more concerned with her own appearance than with the performance of music. Anyway, lipstick is not helpful in tone production.

Choosing Pieces: Play pieces that show what you *can* do and not pieces which demonstrate your deficiencies.

Colleges and universities are concerned with potential. Most candidates *believe* that the panel is concerned with interpretation. The performance of the music, including interpretation, is a subject *taught* at colleges and universities and at a high level. The panel wants to hear the standard reached by the candidate in technique, tone, articulation and musical potential so as to assess the chances of the applicant reaching a reasonable performing standard within three or four years. An applicant should demonstrate a Proper grounding in the building blocks of performance.

Music College or University? Colleges of music and universities differ in their audition requirements, so these will be dealt with separately. However, in choosing which kind of musical education is required, remember that colleges of music in the UK are broadly concerned with performance, and universities with studying music, though this is not true in other countries. Both train teachers, though universities have increasingly, during the past few years, put more emphasis on performance. Some universities have performance courses of which at least one third of the total course is spent on the principal instrument. Mostly this has been due to the increase in the numbers of good players who haven't found places at a college of music.

In deciding which is the most suitable course, weigh up these factors:

a) A music college has teachers better equipped to teach performing than are generally found at universities.

b) Music colleges have student players of a higher standard than at a university; this can provide stimulus and competition for would-be performers.

c) Music colleges have orchestras of a good standard, an important point for those hoping to embark on an orchestral career.

d) A university offers a wider education, which may increase the chances of the graduate gaining employment.

e) A prospective employer may be more impressed with a good university degree than with a performing diploma, or graduate diploma, from a music college.

People do go to universities and graduate as performers; some take a postgraduate course at a music college. There are many applicants who, not having been offered a place at a music college, assert that they will still go all out for a performing career at a suitable university.

The whole problem needs to be looked at from a purely practical point of view. About 35 young would-be performers are offered places at the six principal colleges of music in the United Kingdom each year. Each college auditions about 80 applicants and some offer 2 or 3 places, some about 8. Altogether in 1987 about 150-200 prospective performers applied to colleges.

Case Histories – Mr A and Miss B: Mr A auditions for four colleges and is offered a place at one of them and a 'reserve' place at two others. In the national batting order for that year, out of all the flute players auditioned, he is number 26.

Mr A, even though he has gained a place at a college as a performer, is unlikely to succeed in that aim because, in his particular year, there are 25 people who, in the opinion of the different audition panels, are potentially better than he. Those 25 won't sit about during their first year waiting for Mr A to catch up. *Mr A is unlikely to catch up.* The better equipped the student is on arrival, the more likely he is to progress at a faster rate than the less well equipped.

Four years later, as he is soon to graduate from college, Mr A is assessing his chances of employment (unless he, like so many others, puts off the evil day by taking a postgraduate course). He *may* have climbed up the ladder a little or slipped back down. He will never know unless he has the chance to compare his own performing skills with those of his contemporaries. (See 'Summer Schools'.) Generally, though, Mr A thinks he is quite a good player and believes his chances of gaining work in an orchestra are high.

What Mr A hasn't considered is that when 35 players go to colleges of music, 35 players have also left, not to mention the many who have left universities, polytechnics and less prestigious music colleges, perhaps hoping, too, to perform. In the UK, the performing branch of music can absorb no more than around 10 players per year. Mr A isn't going to be one of them unless he has some unusual skill. For many young applicants, the fact that a college of music has offered them a place appears to rubber stamp their future as a performer. Nothing could be further from the truth.

Musicianship combined with Proper flute playing isn't a matter of learning and memorizing facts. Neither, one supposes, are most other professions, though many, like medicine, rely on the ability to remember and recall a vast amount of information at any given moment.

Music needs a special kind of ability and talent, a good instinct, intelligence combined with personal warmth and, above all, the desire, the need, the *want*, to communicate those feelings through the medium of the flute.

To fool most of the people most of the time is not difficult. The music profession contains many who make a good living at it.

Mr A, when he first expressed a desire to go to a music college, may have felt a subconscious instinct *not* to find out what the opposition was like. It might have put him off. He is happier with his dreams.

Miss B feels strongly about music, and flute playing as a profession. She applies for an advice audition at a college of music. She is told that she has a chance but only a slim one, unless she starts practising three or more hours a day and obtains good lessons with a Proper teacher who is aware of current standards. Miss B feels alarmed but determined. How does she increase her practice time from a previous thirty minutes to at least three hours? Her schoolteachers insist that success in life is measured in terms of academic achievement. She has just been told, at her advice audition, that the music profession isn't interested in academic grades; she only needs the basic educational requirement *in order to get a grant*. What will get her into a music college isn't being a good girl at school and completing all her homework and projects neatly and on time. It is being flutistically head and shoulders above the competition. Not interpretation, or the choice of pieces; purely and simply, a good standard of playing and a high musical potential. A Proper flute player.

Miss B attends a summer school where she hears, and talks to, many players of about her own age. Some are better flute players, some not so good. She finds out which colleges have a reputation for flute playing and the best teachers to ask for. She goes home, puts away her Bach Sonatas and starts practising technical exercises and studies.

She needs to, because all the serious opposition is doing likewise and Miss B is determined to be better than them all.

Miss B is realistic.

Audition Requirements: Music colleges offer courses to talented players who have already achieved a high standard of performance. They are not there to act as hospitals to cure all the ills that the applicant has acquired through lack of practice, basic playing faults, or poor teaching. Most players do, however, have some faults which need correcting. The audition panel weighs up the handicaps against the plus points. Too many handicaps, such as bad posture or hand positions, embouchure problems, poor technique, wrong fingering, poor sound, articulation problems, all weigh heavily against acceptance. If the candidate were accepted, it would mean perhaps two years putting right the basic playing technique. There's not enough time for that; four years at a college goes by all too quickly.

Universities offer a wide variety of courses, some with a strong bias towards performance and some, too, with good teachers. It is important to ask around and read the prospectuses. Some offer the fees for lessons outside the university, and will pay the cost of travel to get there. If the applicant wants to achieve a good level of performance but, realistically, knows what the competition is like, then he should take all the available opportunities. Some applicants have the idea that although they haven't obtained a place at a college of music, they will re-apply after university, for a postgraduate course at a music college. Most colleges offer one or two places per year at post-graduate level, but often, the college's own students *are also competing for these places.* The chances are that the standard will be very high. All the same, a university can offer a wide musical education and can frequently offer a tailor-made course for a student who has a particular interest, such as early music, or contemporary music performance. Beware, though! Time was when it was thought that those who couldn't put two decent notes together specialized either in early music or contemporary music, or became president of the Students' Union!

I mentioned earlier 'less prestigious music colleges'. A phrase which demands explanation. Apart from the half-dozen well-known colleges of music, there are some very pleasant places to study: amongst them polytechnics and schools of music. The working atmosphere in these institutions is usually very friendly and helpful. They don't often attract the highest level of candidates but are in the business of training instrumentalists and at the same time providing a wider education than, say, a performance course at a larger college. Many graduates become instrumental teachers and a few perform.

Entrance Auditions: Whatever audition is being undertaken, be prepared for anything. Applicants sometimes feel hard done by when scales are requested or when an unprepared piece is put in front of them. "I wasn't warned about this", they say.

It's the panel's job to find out as much as possible about a candidate to ensure that huge sums of public or private money are going to be well spent. Too often, the applicant offers two slow movements from two separate works. When asked to play another of the movements, they reply,

"Oh, I haven't looked at it". What kind of musician would only look at a slow movement, ignoring the other two or three? One who can't play them, the panel suspects. It's tantamount to saying to the panel, "I have no technique".

Be prepared to play a whole work.

Learn all your scales. Not the local examinations variety: only the technically handicapped take those seriously at this stage. Learn the scales through the entire compass of the flute.* A two-octave scale amounts to a declaration of your unfamiliarity with parts of the normal compass of the flute.

A serious flute student would interest himself and be familiar with records and radio broadcasts of flute recitals, with players of different countries, and with what is going on in the international flute world.** He would also have learned a wide variety of pieces.

The interview which generally follows on from an audition is an attempt to find out more about the personality of the applicants. Are they the performing type? What other interests have they? Can they communicate? *Look the interviewer in the eyes, and talk.*

Ask questions about the course for which you are applying, what it entails, which teacher you might get, etc. Don't ask the time of the next train to Newquay.

Orchestral Auditions:*** It may surprise many people to know that out of a hundred auditioned, there are usually up to a dozen capable players, any one of whom would be suitable for the job whether it be principal, subprincipal, or piccolo seats. But to secure an orchestral position requires being head and shoulders above the competition.

Applicants are requested to play one or two solos with piano, and then some prepared and unprepared sight-reading. Choose solos to show how good you are. That is to say, the piece must demonstrate your abilities in a lot of areas: tone, technique, etc, as well as your suitability for an orchestral chair.

In applying for the position of second flute, how do you play the Prokofiev Sonata as a second flute? Well, you don't. But at the same time, to play it very loudly − apart from being unmusical − would be telling the panel that you would be unable − or unwilling − to play under, and balance with, the principal flute.

Be prepared to switch off your vibrato. Be prepared, in fact, for anything! The conductor, the leader, and the principal players, both flute and oboe, vary in their ideas and ideals. It would be hard to please them all. It is a good idea to listen to the principal player on the radio, or at a concert, to get an idea of how best you could fit in.

Principal players won't be interested in you if you are competing with them; they will only see you as a threat. A second flute is a supporting role in many ways, not least of which is allowing the principal player to play at his ease, and to assist him. Only a silly second flute would be practising the 'big tune' in the dressing room before the concert, especially so within the hearing of the principal.

I have had the pleasure of knowing personally a very nice man whom I shall refer to as Mr X. He was the second flute in a symphony orchestra in which I was casually employed as principal. He normally played a wooden flute, but changed on my arrival to a silver one, saying nothing about it. (I found out later from one of the string players.)

At the first concert − a 'live' broadcast − there was only one flute required. Mr X sat on the platform with me, and when I took a breath to play (in fact a wrong entry), he put his hand on my knee and said quietly "Next bar". He did this on a few other occasions, too, when he

*See *Practice Book 5 − Scales* − page 24.
**The British Flute Society is helpful here as, of course, are other national flute societies in other countries.
***See also CONCERTS AND COMPETITIONS in this book.

had himself no reason to count my bars' rests. He was a quietly unassuming man who created a relaxed atmosphere in which one tried one's best. He sometimes murmured charming compliments. What was really strange was that, by modern standards he was a poor flute player, though he did his job competently. For me, he was the ideal second flute. He will not be remembered as a great player, but I will remember him.

So, there is plenty of choice from the many who audition. It still comes down, in the end, to finding the one who has that 'special something'. Frequently, it is the one who has had the most experience. How does an ex-college graduate gain experience? It's a chicken and egg situation, but there is a way out: the applicant should study the scores, learn the parts and listen both to live concerts and gramophone records in order to gain the experience of what it *feels* and *sounds* like to actually *play* all the tunes.

Most players at auditions play the excerpts very well, but play them in a way which sounds as if *they are completely unaware of what the rest of the orchestra is doing.* This is a bad mistake to make. And worse, it isn't difficult for the panel to pinpoint the problem, and, therefore, to eliminate this candidate.

Be prepared for anything, such as being asked to play as softly as possible, and then to repeat the passage at half the volume again! Of course, intonation is very important, too. Cut out unnecessary choreography: wriggling and writhing around will disturb the rest of the woodwind.

What the panel is looking for is someone who will fit in with the woodwind team, not someone who is so individual that they would stick out; there must be at the same time some musical character and personality.

Summer Schools, Camps and Master Classes: Around the world there are many flute courses, master classes and summer camps which can be a valuable source of information, whether it's the latest ideas on playing, flute gadgetry, repertoire or simply meeting others with like interests. The most valuable to the pre-college, college, university or postgraduate player, is the master class where there are lots of flute players. For the 16 or 17 year old, it can provide much valuable information on the current standard of players of the same age, and provide a good kick in the trousers to the lazy and self-satisfied.

To a young player, the importance of rubbing shoulders in their formative years with lots of flute players cannot be too strongly stressed. Just listening to others, whether being taught or not, is a very valuable experience. Such a visit can result in decisive action. One young player will have decided, after a week at such a class, that he will look elsewhere other than flute playing for his career; another will start practising four times as much as before. Both decisions are valuable, because they are the result of realism about a performing career.

The summer schools also allow the young player to meet the well-known artist, to duck him in the swimming pool and beat him at table tennis. It's altogether a good leveller.

THE PICCOLO

The piccolo has been comprehensively covered in the piccolo *Practice Book*,⋆ and there is little to add save that it is a pity that more flute players who have a natural leaning towards the piccolo don't take it up seriously. There is, and always will be, room in the orchestral world for a good piccolo player.

THE BAROQUE FLUTE

In the past, rather cranky people have been known to take up the Baroque flute; maybe failed Boehm flute players or even failed musicians. Not so now. It's a very specialized subject and takes as much time, training and effort as it does to play the Boehm flute. You don't need to be dressed in long flowery clothes, wear sandals, be a vegetarian, or be a devotee of some eastern philosophy in order to play the Baroque flute.

At the time of writing there doesn't seem to be any entry into the Baroque flute world other than by starting on the Boehm flute. This is a pity because it's the wrong way round! But slowly the scene is changing. Not any more 'us and them'; the gap is being filled by conical-bore Boehm flute players at one end, and four-keyed and eight-keyed players at the other. There are even a few who play all types of flute with almost equal facility. And why not? Different they are, but not that different.

At one time, "I'm going to specialize" was a smug reply to a parent's or a teacher's query about future prospects. Now, to diversify is more the order of the day. This trend is a return to the eighteenth century where musicians played many different instruments with great facility, not merely those of the same closely related family.

Colleges and universities are offering specialist courses for the proper study of early music and dance. This will, in time, spread outwards from these establishments, and find its way into schools and local evening classes.

⋆Patricia Morris and Trevor Wye, *A Piccolo Practice Book* (Novello).

BAROQUERY

CONTEMPORARY OR EXTENDED
FLUTE TECHNIQUES

A better phrase, 'extended', than all the previous words used to express the often curious sounds emitted by those who study these techniques. Most of the new techniques are, in fact, simply extensions of existing ones, including circular breathing, itself a very old technique indeed.

It used to be said that the kinds of noises made in contemporary music are the sounds one has been assiduously avoiding throughout one's performing career. That was in its early days. It now needs to be taken more seriously. More and more, the young professional is required to play multiphonics, notes in the fourth octave, and the many timbres made possible by the use of special fingerings. There are those who aren't satisfied by the number of possibilities on the existing Boehm flutes and wish to add holes – and keys to cover them – in order to increase the range of possibilities.

Colleges haven't caught on to this fascinating subject in quite the same way as they have with early music; indeed, some ignore it altogether. No doubt this is, at any rate in part, due to the awful gestation period contemporary music went through in the Fifties and Sixties when many who had no idea of Clementi, let alone Mozart, plugged into Haubenstock-Ramati and John Cage with great glee. Here was music which didn't require 'a beautiful tone' or even the right notes.

I can remember during one most unmemorable piece asking the conductor/composer out of sheer frustration and bloody-mindedness, "Who has the tune?". I can also remember several occasions where, at South Bank concerts in London, various orchestral rebels let fly with distorted snatches of Colonel Bogey – and not Kenneth Alford's version either!

Extended technique specialists have appeared in recent years and have written books about their subject, a list of which can be found in the Bibliography.

EXPRESSION, PHRASING AND STYLE

Expression: Marcel Moyse had a rule: "Play the music and not the flute". Having learned all the nuts and bolts of flute technique, this rule is the main crossroads which can decide the outcome of a player's career. Up one road lies the subjugation of self and one's ego, and the search for the right way to portray the composer's intentions. That's interpretation.

Up another road is the desire to express *oneself*, regardless of the music. This road is easier: it involves allowing the music to take second place and giving reign to one's personal feelings and emotions regardless of what the music is trying to say. That's conceit.

The composer writes a piece; you, the performer, consider it to be a good piece. On what grounds? Because it allows you to express yourself? What is it that you feel the need to express? Boy/girlfriend troubles? Your unhappy childhood? A row at school?

Who cares? No one.

It seems a curious kind of event where you sell tickets to 250 people who expect to hear the Poulenc Sonata and hear instead a musical portrait of your current emotional problems.

A composer is rather like an architect who designs a cathedral. The architect makes detailed drawings of every part of his building; it would be a foolish stonemason who decided to carve different windows – he would lose his job. If the cathedral is truly beautiful, then it is the stonemason's job to execute the carvings according to the design of the architect. If the stonemason disagrees with the plans, he should design his own and declare himself as the architect.

Music is like this. We have been left blueprints for performance and our job is to put life into those designs if we respect the work of the composer. Of course, it's not always as simple as that. Many is the time when you believe there is a misprint in the music; keyholes don't usually fit on the hinge side of a door. And sometimes, even though you have tried hard to justify it, the *crescendo* to *forte* doesn't seem to give the right effect; so you change it.

Some of our own personality is sure to appear in the music: but it is *not the principal objective in performance*. Sometimes, we choose pieces because they show off what we are good at doing. OK, but don't revolve the whole of a performance around your loud low C. *A Proper flute player will play the music, not the flute.*

Phrasing: Phrasing is the art of shaping a melody by stress and articulation. It needs to be studied, not as the result of intellectual analysis but as the result of genuine musical feeling. Authors and composers have phrases, grammar, paragraphs and sentences to consider, as architects have bricks, mortar, windows, doors and buttresses. It has been said that the barline is there for the beginner; the duty of the artist is to *overcome* the barline.

The object of phrasing is to express correctly a musical idea. That alone, though, isn't sufficient to make the phrase beautiful. Further, a series of 'correctly' played phrases aren't enough for the player to claim a truly musical performance.

During the first half of this century, music of whatever period often had the same performing treatment; it was called a 'line'. Only during the 1880s did the 'long line' phrase come into being with the music of Richard Wagner, whose long lines often stretched for an entire opera and even on to breakfast the next day! These long lines are not relevant to music written before 1880. There *is* a line, but it is achieved by different means.

Music flows forwards. To achieve this we use various musical devices such as crescendo, vibrato changes and perhaps accelerando to take us to these high points. But these devices, applied mechanically, don't give any kind of satisfactory musical performance; they sound like tricks.

Nevertheless, these 'tricks' need to be studied as part of the basic building blocks in Proper phrasing. To arrive at any satisfactory musical result, you should play this way because you *love it* and *believe in it*, not because you read it in this, or any other book.

At some time or another we all study form, though this seems to have little relevance to performance. Of course it has, but the performer's desire to express himself takes the upper hand − or to put it another way, we express ourselves instead of the music. A sonata is a complete cathedral: it has a nave, chancel, choir, chapter house, and the rest. To build it so that the parts complement each other in the overall design is difficult, but the building processes start with the foundations, the building blocks of basic phrasing.

A rule: the first beat of the bar is the most important beat; the remainder are, therefore, weaker. In a phrase ending:

the quaver, or quarter note, G must be weaker than the quaver A. To play both with the same loudness is crude. Like saying qua*ver*. There is a natural bounce from strong to weak.

Similarly, lightening the second note applies even when it goes up:

That's more difficult because, as mentioned before, the natural tendency is to play louder on the flute when ascending.

In the phrase:

the music should progress (crescendo, move forward) to the first beat of the second bar, and then diminuendo. If it doesn't do this, the effect is clumsy. The second bar will sound like tender*ly*. What is more important is that, if it is played in this way to audition panelists, judges at competitions, and audiences, *we haven't learnt the basic ABC of phrasing*; our playing is *crude, clumsy* and *unmusical*. We are not Proper flute players.

So, it is better to practise some simple studies in order to discover in which direction the phrase should go, the basics of phrasing.

Marcel Moyse wrote some studies for this very purpose, the *24* and *25 Little Melodious Studies* (Leduc, Paris). Although these books are often used by teachers in order to study all the basic technical and musical devices likely to be found in flute music, they were written for more advanced players, and for the same reason – phrasing. When practising them, look to where you are going, and where you have come *from*. Then you won't ever be guilty of mistakes such as:

which should of course sound more like:

in the Mozart Concerto in D.

It is not necessary to give pages of examples, these three quoted will surely be understood as basic to the understanding of Proper phrasing.

Tied and Dotted Notes: Habits acquired when we are young are hard to lose. A beginner learns to play notes on the beat and, soon after, between the beats. The teacher counts one, two *and* three, in an effort to help. Thereafter, the loud '*and*' denotes an accent.

The second half of the second beat – the 'dot' – has been deliberately subdued by the composer; to reinstate it by an accent is to go against the composer's wishes.

The same rule applies when the phrase goes across a barline, as in:

especially so if the composer has placed any kind of stress, or accent over the first note:

If the composer had wanted:

then the tie would not be written and, of course, the second D, the first beat of the bar, would be the strongest note of the phrase.

Should an advanced performer 'bump' unmusically in a legato phrase, it is tantamount to demonstrating to his audience that he *has* learnt to count; hardly likely to win approbation, or prizes.

Syncopation: The word 'syncopation' derives from *syncope*, which means to faint or swoon. The normal time accents are in conflict with the syncopated accents. Why faint? Because the normal time accents – the heart beat – are interrupted temporarily by the syncopation; the life of a person is similarly interrupted by a faint or swoon. The heart misses a beat. To replace the missing beat by an accent is to remove the whole idea of syncopation.

In the passage:

the E flat is syncopated; to accent the second half of the E flat is to ruin the whole effect of it:

Before swooning or fainting, or indeed any sort of minor interruption to the normally smooth flow of life, we take a breath. More than that, we *accent* the beginning of anything from a sigh to a scream of pain. Further still, the sigh or scream has a *diminuendo*.

Those, then, are the basic ingredients of the syncopation:

a) Take a breath before it.
b) Accent the syncopated note.
c) Make a diminuendo.
d) Don't shorten the syncopated notes.

There *are* exceptions to these rules, but they should be understood as a guide.

If a series of syncopated notes is encountered, then it should have the same treatment:

A breath is always taken – or a space allowed for it – at the start of a syncopated passage:

Syncopation introduces a breathless and emotional atmosphere to the music; the Proper flute player understands this.

These, then, are some of the basic rules of phrasing. Try to create a flow of notes rather than an exhibition of good rhythm. Study simple melodies; they are the key to future progress. After all, fast pieces are simply slow melodies played quickly; they are no less expressive.

Style: In the earlier part of this century, musicians would play the music of all periods in much the same way. The musicians of the 1920s and 30s weren't ignorant; they just didn't have access to the information we have now. Today, there's a subtle difference: it is ignorant to know but not to use the information.

We now understand much more about the different periods of musical style.

The eighteenth- and nineteenth-century rules or customs are simply a record of how music was played at the time. The composer *wrote* in that climate of current usage; he didn't necessarily write for us. So, we need to have some knowledge of the periods of musical history in order to arrive at a beautiful musical result.

A good method of acquiring the atmosphere of another period in musical history is to read books about other subjects in the same period, whichever interests you the most: art, furniture, history, politics, biographies of musicians or important people, jewellery, porcelain, musical instruments, architecture, contemporary diarists, and many more.

Listening to good players on period instruments – not just the flute – can also be very rewarding. In fact, to gather a lot of background 'feel' about, say, eighteenth-century music, the harpsichord repertoire is wonderfully rich. The phrasing, ornaments and style have to be clearly stated on that instrument which largely lacks the means of playing loudly and softly.

String music of the 'authentic' variety is another useful source. One learns quickly that vibrato has to be controlled and often switched off because the music doesn't need it. Can you do that? Vibrato is an ornament. We have become accustomed to non-stop vibrato rather like chips-with-everything. That is a present-day convention. It wasn't the convention throughout the eighteenth and nineteenth centuries. How do we know that? Writers of the different periods have commented on it, but the music often seems to lead us to the same conclusion: a constant wobble gets in the way. A student should learn how to control vibrato. There are plenty of exercises and advice in *Practice Book 4*. Our present convention is to use vibrato all the time, and its absence can sound odd if it is removed *without substituting a different mode of expression suitable to the period*.

What follows is a brief outline of the styles of the three main musical periods of interest to young flute players. It is beyond the scope of this book to draw more than a mere sketch.

Eighteenth-Century Music: For the general reader, he can't do better than to look at Thurston Dart's *The Interpretation of Music* (Hutchinson) for a general survey of eighteenth-century style.

The ease with which we can travel today, together with radio broadcasts and gramophone records, tends to smooth out the difference in national schools of style. Those differences in the eighteenth century were more marked, but were still influenced by players from other countries. We tend to gather together the musical history of all countries and decades into one heap and call it 'the eighteenth century'.

Contemporary eighteenth-century writers provide a lot of information on how to play their music and flutes. We have some 'records' too, in the form of musical boxes and mechanical organs. There are also plenty of instruments around, which give an idea of how they sounded. All of this helps, but our final guide must be whether it sounds good to our ears. Authenticity, for its own sake, is a false god.

Music of the eighteenth century can be played on modern flutes, but the performance should reflect the customs and conventions of the period. Today's louder flutes should be played with circumspection in order to match the silvery delicacy of a French harpsichord. Proper players should learn to match their flute sound to that of the keyboard.

The modern piano seems to portray the spirit of some music far better than the harpsichord can. The Bach Sonatas with obbligato keyboard parts, and some C.P.E. Bach Sonatas are examples. The singing tone of a good modern piano more nearly matches that of today's flute and enables the three-part writing to be heard more clearly.

In sonata playing, it is a mistake to use a cello with the piano: the piano doesn't need it. If a cellist is employed as a continuo player with a harpsichord, then he must be very discreet, or the full, round tone of a modern cello will provide too much bass.

The average player can get to grips with the general style by understanding the way music was phrased then. A new language of phrasing has to be learned. The signs, too, used in music had a different meaning from that to which we are accustomed. The 'time words' (e.g. *Allegretto*) had different interpretations. 'Take the tempo more from the piece than from the time word' (Quantz). Another writer in 1771 wrote 'Taste is the true metronome'.

C.P.E. Bach wrote that the appoggiatura is the most important ornament; it creates tension and release. Baroque music, then, is all about the principle of conflict.

French and Italian music differed both in compositional style and in performance. 'The French in their airs aim at the soft, the easy, the flowing and the coherent', whereas, 'the Italians venture at everything that is harsh and out of the way' for 'as the Italians are naturally much more brisk than the French, so they are more sensible of the passions'. In France they play 'much finer and with greater nicety' (Raguenet, 1709).

In Italian music everything is carefully notated; in French music more interpretation is required. For example, although a musical passage is written evenly, the right rhythm has to be interpreted. Degrees of inequality − called inégale − can vary a lot. Good taste dictated how much.

Performers were much closer to, and shared more common ground with composers than in later history and were expected to add graces, to ornament, improvise at sight, and accompany from a figured bass by the application of good taste, not always by the written note.

The differences aren't confined merely to the right ornaments, or the right instruments: they are more fundamental than that. Musical style grew out of the social custom and atmosphere of the time. There wasn't a set of arbitrary rules. No one sat down and wrote out a list of ornaments or embellishments. Least of all did they say that 'as from today all trills will start on the upper note . . . except sometimes'. Books were written about style just as this book is being written now: *it's a record of this author's current belief and practice.*

In eighteenth-century music, then, there are conventions and customs with which we should become familiar. They are part of the overall musical concept in the same way that Gothic windows belong to Gothic buildings. A Gothic building with aluminium and plate glass windows looks daft. Just as the style of speech and style of dress was different then, so too was the music.

It's not so difficult to find out about this period: there are so many records and concerts that, with an open mind, and a willingness to learn, a lot can be achieved. 'A musician cannot move others unless he too is moved' (C.P.E. Bach).

The Classical Period: The dominant role which the flute enjoyed during the eighteenth century went into decline. None of the major composers, Haydn, Mozart or Beethoven, wrote a sonata for flute and piano. (The Mozart Sonatas K.10 − 15 are for piano and flute or violin.)* Composers wrote sonatas for the piano with a flute accompaniment, the piano taking the primary role. There were still twice as many works composed for the flute than for any of the other woodwind.

Flute duets too became more common. Swept away were all the frills, embellishments and baroquery of the previous era. The figured bass, too, gradually disappeared.

The flute repertoire in this period is rather thin, though new pieces are constantly appearing in publishers' catalogues. Mozart, Haydn and Gluck are our chief sources of repertoire for concerts.

Mozart is difficult, we are often informed. Technically, this is not true; musically it has some foundation. The problem lies within the listener. Mozart's three concertos and the quartets are truly beautiful, which makes them more sensitive to phrasing and expression errors, not to mention wrong notes. The Mozart lover is wounded by a poor performance. Like the Bach Sonatas, players will disagree about interpretation (the competition performer of Mozart has a difficult task!). This shouldn't in any way deter the performer from playing Mozart, though he may be circumspect about where he plays it.

The problem facing the performer is that the music of this era, with its simple lines and construction, is nearer to our 'long line' concept of phrasing which appeared in the late nineteenth century.

*The authenticity of the Beethoven Sonatas is in doubt.

The performer often mistakenly treats earlier music in this way.

For example, the Mozart Flute Concertos* have few written crescendos and diminuendos, the reason being that the slur is the *equivalent* of a diminuendo. Cadenzas, we know, were usually short, limited to the available breath of the player, unlike the flights of fancy often heard in today's concerts.

The modern flutist should be free to change the articulation because of the different size of tone of today's flutes. In general, the Baroque and Classical flutes project better when slurring less. The modern flute should slur more than indicated on the original copy, unless the part has already been edited in that way.

Style is such a difficult subject: there were so many styles. All one can do is to follow the copy faithfully and change what was written only if the music and its performance are enhanced by so doing.

Nineteenth-Century Music: The music of Doppler, Demersseman and Tulou are once again re-appearing on the concert platform and can be a rewarding source of repertoire. This music is often dismissed as silly and exaggerated, but it was written in a period when the flute's range of available notes was extended and, together with the new keywork mechanism of Boehm and others, enabled players to whizz around more easily. Much of the music was written for amateur amusement but there are some delightful solos to be found amongst all the nonsense. The trick of this music is to wear your heart unashamedly on your sleeve. Let go. Charm and astonish your audience.

In the second half of the nineteenth century, it was OK to have a nude statue or nude portrait in your home; it wasn't OK to display an ankle – even the piano legs were sometimes covered! This seems prudish to us, but all that suppressed emotion was allowed to reveal itself in heart-rending, emotional tunes. Bravery and courage were looked upon as ideals for the gentlemen (ladies rarely played the flute; it was said that the reason was they couldn't talk and play the flute at the same time!). So we have courageous bravura solos to be played with bristling moustaches and a fiery technique.

These big pieces – the six Concert Solos of Demersseman are a good example – have to be played really well to get across to an audience. A flute player who tackles these works seriously has to be an actor, comedian, romantic lover, and a virtuoso performer all rolled into one. The long – sometimes overlong – introductions are important stage setters; you need an imaginative pianist. After fifty bars the soloist enters, sometimes coyly from the wings, sometimes with a bravura declamation. After some whizzing around there is a quiet and gentle melody, full of vocal tricks. A cadenza or two with fearsome swoops which leads to the brilliant final tune written in a way which sounds like two parts played simultaneously. The coda, covering the entire compass, results in thunderous applause.

The playing of an *Adagio* was a study in itself, and considered to be an important attribute of a virtuoso.

Some of the special effects possible on the eight-keyed flute are no longer available to us on our modern instruments, a good example being the glide. This was used to connect two notes smoothly and involved a glissando in the manner used by many singers. Our open-holed flutes allow some gliding but not quite in the way Nicholson would have played it.

The basic scale of the eight-keyed flute is D major: that is, removing one finger at a time from the low end, it plays the scale of D. Our Boehm flutes are, of course, based on D minor. No wonder, then, that much of the D and G major rapid passage work was much easier on the eight-keyed flute than on our flutes.

The solos of Louis Drouet give us a clue as to the kind of sound made in the 1840s. These formidable pieces must be technically amongst the very hardest of all flute music ever written.**

*Novello & Co. Ltd.

**See *God Save the King* (Variations) and others (Broekmans & van Poppel).

They contain leaps of an octave or more to be played at terrifying speeds. How did Drouet do it? In the answer to that lies some interesting information which can be of use to us in deciding upon what kind of sound we want to make on present-day flutes.

We shall look at three well-known flute players from around 1840 about whose playing and style something is known.

Firstly, Charles Nicholson, who had a powerful tone and whose *Adagios* were much admired. He doubtless played with the blow-hole well uncovered and the head pulled out.

Louis Drouet had a smaller, sweeter tone and a formidable technique. He frequently performed his own (almost impossible) works.

Theobald Boehm's style lies between the two: a good technique with a medium-sized tone.

A performer usually writes music which he is then asked to perform. Nicholson wrote countless airs and variations, the variations of which were readily accessible to most players. They didn't leap about at breakneck speed, unlike Drouet's. Boehm's works contain big leaps but not the impossible.

Boehm once wrote to W.S. Broadwood, an English player, saying 'I always draw out the head a little, not as much as some, but never pushed right in'. With the head pushed right in, the flute would have to be turned in to flatten an otherwise sharp intonation. With the head pulled out − à la Nicholson − the flute would have to be turned out to raise the pitch. Turning the headjoint out increases the dynamic range and at the same time, renders octave playing, and other leaps, more difficult.

We can, therefore, conclude that Drouet must have had a small tone − with the headjoint turned in − in order to be able to play those double octave leaps with the rapidity with which he was reputedly credited. To play Drouet's solos today, on Boehm flutes capable of an overall larger tone and with the fashionable requirements of a modern symphony orchestra, is considerably more difficult than it would be on a Drouet eight-keyed flute.

The nineteenth-century player was accustomed to wearing his heart on his sleeve; he strived to charm *and* to astonish. Much of nineteenth-century music should, therefore, be uninhibited, warm and extrovert both in the *Adagio* and in the rapid passage work. If the modern flute player feels embarrassed by this honest sentiment, then he shouldn't play music of this period − it will only sound stiff and cold. This may account for the lack of popularity amongst audiences for nineteenth-century flute music.

These solos are, after all, rather like entire operas for flute and piano, complete with a prima donna. Some flute players consider much of the nineteenth-century repertoire just a joke. Moyse used to say, "Play it first − laugh afterwards".

That means, *really* play it.

The Impressionists and After: The flute repertoire is rich in music from the first quarter of this century, especially French music.

This music is particularly vulnerable to mis-reading, mis-interpretation and mistakes. Where possible, avoid listening to a new piece on a record or cassette during the process of learning it. It's better to get to grips with what the composer wrote first, and then listen later. Learn a new piece accurately first. If necessary, use a metronome even with solo pieces such as Debussy's *Syrinx* and Ibert's *Pièce*. In that way, the printed rhythms will be appreciated before any rubato is added.

It's necessary to play in time before robbing it. As someone once remarked, you spend your first few years learning how to play in time; the next few learning to play out of time.

For example, we can listen to a recording of Debussy's *Syrinx* and, after, unconsciously play what we *think* we hear. The ebbing and flowing, the rubato, is remembered when we actually read the notes. It results in a distorted performance based on another performer's imagination.

It is so easy to play what we *think* is there on the page; a closer examination often reveals something quite different.

Look at a copy of *L'Après Midi d'un Faune* by Debussy. The composer wrote:

Reproduced by permission of Editions Jobert, Paris/UMP.

The fifth beat – in **9/8** – contains a duplet. How many players play the B natural as part of the triplet which follows?

In Honneger's *Danse de la Chèvre*, the third and fourth bars are written:

Reproduced by permission of Editions Salabert, Paris/UMP.

In bar 4, there is a duplet followed by a triplet. How many performers play the F natural as part of the following triplet?

Mistakes are easily made and reflect the player's wish to play what he *thinks* is there, not what is in fact written. Duplets and triplets, or dotted notes mixed with triplets are a feature of this period of music. See also Enesco, Gaubert, Huë and others. Maybe it doesn't sound important? To anyone who knows and loves these works, it *is* important.

SYRINX

It's easy to dab away at the musical canvas to create 'effects'. The results are the performer's 'effects', not the composer's. As musical history advances, it becomes more difficult to play precisely what is on the printed page, especially so in the past three decades.

One day in the 1930s, so the story goes, the BBC Symphony Orchestra were rehearsing a new work which everyone had difficulty in reading. The principal flute was engrossed in a magazine when his second flute asked him "Aren't you going to look at the next passage? It looks very difficult". "No," the principal replied. "Aren't you worried that you might play some wrong notes?" he was asked. "No," he replied, "it's just as easy to play the right ones."

The techniques used in avant-garde music are dealt with very capably by others.★ The new techniques and the music may come hard to the newcomer, but can be rewarding in the long term. As in other periods of history, out of the morass of musical junk – what's known as squeaky-gate music – there are some real gems which are well worth the time and effort spent in learning them.

★See the Bibliography.

Before buying any contemporary flute piece, the Proper flute player will first ascertain whether the work is *worth* learning – especially when these new techniques take so much effort and time to learn. He can do this by asking other players, by looking at the repertoire lists for summer schools and music camps, and by keeping an eye on programmes played by reputable soloists. Record catalogues can help, too. If a piece is considered to be really good, it will have frequent public exposure.

CONCERTS AND COMPETITIONS

Choosing a Programme: For most competitions, there is usually a choice of works. Choose pieces which really show you at your best; music you believe in, music you love. Show your grasp of different styles, if there is a wide choice. It's good competition training to put yourself in the shoes of a judge. What is he looking for? What recipe makes a winner? What distinguishes a winner from the runners-up? Out of half a dozen fine flute players, how do they select one player as the best?

Assuming that all contestants have broadly the same attributes such as a beautiful tone, fine technique and articulation, and good intonation, it must come down to musical performance. Music is a difficult subject to write or talk about, and to judge. W.H. Auden once wrote 'Aside from purely technical analysis, nothing can be *said* about music, except when it is bad; when it is good, one can only listen and be grateful'. That just about sums it up. Judges usually write about the bad points in a performance, the technical flaws, the intonation, etc. When a performance is musically captivating, they put down their pens, sit back, and enjoy it.

Listeners and judges at competitions most often complain of:

1) Poor intonation; a flat low register and a sharp high register.

2) Little or no dynamic range.

3) Basic technical problems, the most common of which is articulation.

4) An obsession with self, combined with little attempt to convey at least the spirit of what the composer wrote.

5) Lack of communication to the audience.

The winner usually has most of these problems under control, but frequently, the winner is the one who best conveys the sheer delight and enjoyment for the music being performed. That means a strong desire to communicate a love for the music. Don't mix this up with a love for oneself, though that is very necessary too.

Take a layman's view of the flute: it is an instrument with little dynamic range; it plays louder when ascending, softer when descending. Right. Let's change *that* for a start. There are plenty of exercises already mentioned in this book. The clarinet, saxophone, cello, piano and the human voice, in fact *all* musical instruments get louder when descending. The flute doesn't. To change this entails practising tone exercises in order to strengthen the low notes.

Low note strength won't appear like tongues of fire after a blessing from a flute-playing bishop. It comes from trying to play the low notes with depth and strength. The *Practice Book 1* exercises on tone always have a crescendo to the lowest note, and for a very good reason.

Quite a number of competitors have little dynamic variation. That applies to orchestral audition candidates too. Change it. It is within your power to do so.

The other points have been covered in this and in the *Practice Books*.

One final point: no matter how lovely your tone, how brilliant your technique, how stunning your articulation, how astute your musical understanding, you are only as good as your weakest attribute; if you can't end a note without going flat, then goodbye. Next, please.

The answer really is with you, not in this, or in any other book.

Playing from Memory: Competition players are more frequently expected to play without the script, and with good reason. The musical message is easier to convey when there is no 'music reading' in the way.

That only works after you have spent a long time getting accustomed to communicating to an audience without the copy. It needs practice and frequent public exercise before the benefits to the performer are fully appreciated. *Practice Book 5*, pages 45 and 53, offers some practical advice on the subject.

Even if it is not a requirement of the competition, it is always more impressive to judges when the competitor does play from memory.

RECITALISTS AND COMPETITORS

Stage Manner: Looking the part of a recitalist or competitor who recognizes the importance of the occasion is a first priority. Untidy dress shows lack of respect for panel and audience alike. (It may show a lack of respect for oneself, too.)

For professional recitalists the convention for a long time now has been to wear a uniform: black or unobtrusive attire. The pianos too are black. The idea is to create a neutral picture in order to draw the audience's attention away from the performers and thereby to attract attention to the music.

If the judges were to arrive in unsuitable clothing, then their credibility and fitness to judge an important competition might be called into question.

Most judges wouldn't consciously mark down someone for appearing sloppily dressed, but it's difficult to be certain that, when given a choice between A or B, they wouldn't prefer properly dressed A to badly dressed B.

It's not worth taking the chance.

Playing with a Piano: Practise your duo sonata from the piano copy. It is the only part which contains all the information required for a Proper performance. For example:

This passage isn't going to reach the Top Twenty. It's a second violin part. But, combined with the first violin tune below, it could.

If the piano part is truly an *accompaniment*, as opposed to part of a duo, then the pianist takes a secondary role, albeit still an important one.

Most good music is in duo form and some of it, such as the Bach Sonata in B minor, is in trio form: the flute part, the right hand part and the left hand part.

A knowledge of what the pianist plays is essential to Proper musical understanding. This can only be acquired by practising from the full score or piano copy. Even if the ear can't hear all the notes, at the very least, rhythms can be recognized and appreciated when practising by oneself.

Acknowledge the role of the pianist. When you have finished your sonata, bow *with* the pianist. He isn't someone who just happened to be passing the hall at the time of your rehearsal and was conveniently persuaded to play an accompaniment to your big moment. He is *part* of your performance, a big part of it.

Now we recognize the accompanist as an essential part of your duo appearance, don't put a sack over his head and try to hide him: *open the piano lid.* Not the full stick − it is for most players too much, but at least the short stick. If the piano hasn't got one, ask for one to be provided. An ordinary piece of wood the length of a flute case would do admirably.

It's important just once in your performing life to be convinced by this; go into the body of the hall and ask a friend to alternately raise and lower the lid whilst a bit of full-blooded piano playing is in progress. To put the lid down reduces the pianist to a dogsbody rôle. The lid is, anyway, to keep the dust out, not the notes in.

If you are afraid of being overpowered then ask your pianist to play softer, or you should practise your nuances until *you* can play louder.

Judges would see that the closed lid either reflects your non-ability to play loudly; your lack of regard for the role of the pianist; or your ignorance about piano tone. The fully-opened lid can help to reflect the flute tone if the performer stands in the curve of the piano and points the end of his flute toward the lid.

A Proper flute player performs with the piano lid at least partially open.

Bowing: Practise bowing. By oneself. It is embarrassing, but it is all part of the act. A flute player is also in show business and must learn to acknowledge the applause. Try counting when bowing in order not to rush. Watch others, and copy someone's stage manner which you admire.

"AM I TOO LOUD?"

Look at the Audience: As you walk on to the platform, look at your audience. It will help you to get rid of your nervousness. Walk on slowly. Bow slowly. Make certain your partner is ready to bow with you, or it may look as though you are presuming that the applause is all yours. Try to smile. It may only be an act, but so it is.

Speak to the audience. Tell them about the piece. Try not to give a synopsis of the piece, or your views on how lovely it is − you are going to prove that.

It's a good idea to keep your comments to a few sentences without resorting to "Henry Bloggs was born in 1741 and died in Mesopotamia in 1789". Try to find a way of starting obliquely, such as "Antonio Vivaldi died in 1741, the year in which the little-known composer Henry Bloggs was born. Bloggs achieved fame mostly because he was convicted of embezzlement in 1772. His subsequent imprisonment so weakened his health that he died a pauper at the age of 48. This sonata has four movements following the usual pattern of slow-fast slow-fast."

Don't learn what you want to say by heart — it often goes wrong. The written word is quite different to the spoken word. If you read what you have planned to say, it can sound stilted. Think of the basic bones of the message you wish to convey and don't worry about a few stumbles. Practise speaking without using hesitant sounds such as 'ah', or 'er'. You probably know someone who starts off every sentence with "Ah . . . Henry Bloggs . . . ah . . .".

Choreography: C.P.E. Bach suggested it was wrong for a performer to remain perfectly still whilst playing. I wonder what he would have said about some of the weird gyrations to be seen on today's concert platforms. The author has heard of one American university where a student was not only *warned* not to keep still, but was given instructions on *how* to move.

Players do move their bodies as they are moved by the music, but to superimpose a ballet on to the musical presentation is arrogant. Most often, those that move have, musically, little to say; the knees bend to deputize for crescendo and diminuendo; the undulating arms and elbows draw the audience's attention away from the lack of phrasing. Those who move, needn't move!

THE PROPER PUPIL

Lessons: A pupil should be properly prepared for a lesson. That is sometimes difficult but it is important to remember that a teacher can only guide and direct; he cannot effect change without the pupil's co-operation. A teacher can inspire, but the results come from the pupil. Don't waste your teacher's time or your parents' money.

Don't expect that the possession of information alone is sufficient to effect change. Without practice, change won't take place. A teacher expects the pupil to practise the points raised in lessons. Reading this book may give some insights into flute technique but it won't transform it unless practice is done.

If a pupil can't manage to prepare Properly for a lesson, there are a number of things he can do to make the lesson worthwhile, such as taking some pieces along, or being prepared to ask questions. A bad pupil stands, instrument in hand, waiting to be taught. The attitude suggests "Well, here I am, so teach me something". Learning and teaching are a joint effort. If the pupil doesn't really *want* to be taught, then the lesson becomes an act: both teacher and pupil end up playing a role. The wholehearted participation of the pupil is essential for a lesson to have been worthwhile.

Changing Teachers: This has already been discussed in an earlier section (under FINDING A TEACHER: 'Middle Level') but not from the pupil's point of view. For whatever reasons a pupil has to change teachers such as a house move or change of school or job, always give the new teacher a fair try. If a pupil has studied with one teacher for some years, that teacher will always be warm in his memory. The new teacher has the job of trying to match up to the pupil's idea of what a good teacher is. That's a difficult position to start with.

People are different. Most teachers, though broadly offering the same basic advice, communicate to their pupils in different ways. To make comparisons is unfair. To refer frequently to what your previous teacher said on the subject is also unfair and, in fact, bad manners.

Teachers may offer advice which is contrary to what the pupil may have been told by a previous teacher. The new embouchure, hand positions, or whatever, are offered in the light of the pupil's present achievement. This new advice should be followed; to resist creates an intolerable situation. The Proper pupil will encourage his teacher to give of his best.

"My Teacher is No Good": If you are really sure, then change, if that is possible (see the section called FINDING A TEACHER). You should feel that you are able to trust your teacher. If that isn't the situation, then after careful consideration, go elsewhere.

If you are stuck with your teacher for whatever reason, try to find what interests him the most, on the flute or musically, and tap into that subject as often as possible. At least for a time, you will be having worthwhile lessons even though technically one-sided.

The One-Lesson Student: Many of the world's well-known players are asked by the travelling student for one or two lessons, or sometimes for a 'consultation' lesson.

A consultation can be useful to the student who simply wants an opinion on the state of his playing and perhaps some guidance towards improving or correcting faults. It's not possible to *mend* faults at a consultation: the consultant, as in medicine, can only diagnose. He can't instantly cure, though he can offer advice as to where lessons – or cures – can be obtained.

There are 'serious' flute students who travel throughout Europe or the USA having one-off lessons with the mighty. It looks good on a biography and it's a relatively cheap way of meeting the distinguished players and teachers. And it's mostly a complete waste of time, save for the social aspect and the biography. 'Klaus Smith studied with Mr A, B, C, D, E, F and G.' What the writer would like to know is what has Klaus Smith done to all the other teachers that he wants to add *me* to his list of scalps? What can I offer that the others were, presumably, unable to communicate to him? Maybe the student simply wants confirmation that his ability is as good as his own opinion of it.

Some well-known players with whom I have discussed this told me that "All the travelling student wants is praise. So, as they pay well, give it to them".

Studying is a continuing process and can't be seriously undertaken by flitting from teacher to teacher to find the one who most agrees with the pupil. To find the real worth of a teacher, a pupil should be prepared to undertake at least a dozen lessons in order to make a judgement as to their effectiveness.

Teachers – and players – can be moody too; just like students! Only after a period of time spent practising, can a student assess the value of the advice given.

Marcel Moyse used to say "Love and respect your teacher; if you don't – go to someone else!"

A Clash of Personality: The relationship between teacher and pupil is usually much closer than in normal school work. The one-to-one (or perhaps a few more) ratio is partly responsible. More so is the fact that, apart from purely technical matters, the subject being taught – music – is based on emotion. This may heighten the personal relationship between the teacher and the taught.

Some people just don't get on with each other. If the pupil has studied with a particular teacher, and, for whatever reason, doesn't like the lessons, then it may be wise to change to another teacher if that is possible. But before doing so, weigh up the pros and cons: whether you like your teacher or not, is he a *good* teacher? Would the new teacher be as good? Do you want a change because the new teacher is less strict and perhaps works his pupils less?

An artist once told me that he'd had four teachers at college: three were really nice to him and praised him constantly, the other was often unkind. "But," he said, "the last one was by far the best teacher; he was unkind because he really *cared* about me."

THE PROPER TEACHER

Teaching:
> *I demand all that I can.*
> *I always try to demand more.*
> *I feel I never demand enough.*
> *You must expect from them a great constant effort to develop all that*
> *brings them the freedom of expression.*
>
> *NADIA BOULANGER*

The most cruel statement made about teaching is, 'Those who play, do; those who can't, teach'. What nonsense. Teaching is an art; more importantly, some teachers are much better at the art of teaching than many famous solo and orchestral players.

In music colleges, the student who wishes to teach is often looked upon as a failed performer, largely because there is inadequate training for the prospective instrumental teacher, a fact long recognized. The problem starts with colleges accepting more players than the profession can take. Those who don't perform are directed toward what is thought of as a lesser craft, teaching. It shouldn't be regarded like this but currently, it is.

Teaching can be as rewarding and enriching as performing, particularly when the teacher is a good performer and intends to practise both crafts.

Dress: An instrumental teacher should dress properly. His style of dress won't, of course, in any way affect his knowledge, but it may diminish his credibility in the eyes of his pupils. Some pupils may say, "I don't really care how my teacher dresses, as long as he teaches me properly!" The problem is that *some* of his pupils may find fault with his appearance and so too may the parents, who are, after all, paying the fees. A Proper teacher should dress in a way which offends no one.

A good rule is, the more junior and inexperienced a teacher may be, the less he can afford to dress improperly. Untidy dress, unkempt hair, breath smelling of lunchtime beer all diminish credibility.

From the collection of W. Bennett Esq.

TEACHING

Therapist or Teacher? As many experienced teachers will appreciate, one tends to draw a notional line, below which the teacher may suggest to his pupil that he gives up or transfers to another instrument. Some teachers on the other hand, will continue to teach a pupil no matter how ill-fitted for that instrument they are, provided that the pupil *wants* to continue. Therein lies the problem.

The pupil's wishes are, of course, important; so too are the parents who are paying.

During the first year, a Proper teacher will weigh up the factors: the amount of interest shown, the level of natural talent available, and the amount of progress made. The Proper teacher has to look into his crystal ball and predict what level may be reached in, say, five years. If the natural talent and interest in the flute is low, and interest in playing likewise, in five years will it have been worthwhile from the point of view of the parents' purse and the pupil's and teacher's time, to be able to play a slow tune rather badly? It is a dilemma often facing the experienced teacher.

How much will it cost during five years for a flute, flute repairs, music and lessons? Would the pupil have been better off playing something else? Or maybe spending his leisure hours on a hobby for which he has more natural talent and which, therefore, is more likely to be rewarding? (A poor sense of rhythm can be improved; a poor sense of pitch will, in spite of aural training, scarcely change.) A Proper teacher will weigh up all these factors and, in the long-term interest of the pupil, make recommendations accordingly.

Private Teaching Fees: A Proper teacher will charge what he believes is his worth, taking into consideration the current national fees. Various national professional bodies (such as the Incorporated Society of Musicians) make recommendations as to *minimum* fees, and offer a good guideline. To undercharge is, in the long term, foolish: in the eyes of most parents, cheap lessons are less good than more expensive lessons. When a teacher raises his fees he rarely loses pupils. Quite the reverse, for parents will often assume the level of instruction to be higher.

Practice: A teacher will need to keep up his instrumental standard within the time available. Where possible a teacher should timetable himself for daily practice. The standard reached after some years' training or performing, rapidly slips away when the only daily challenge may be the second flute part of *Home on the Range*.

There are many master classes worldwide. A Proper teacher should attend one from time to time to familiarize himself with current standards and trends, not to mention flutes and repertoire. This experience can be a shock, especially as the performing standard of young players is increasing year by year. When the teacher is only exposed to the playing of his own pupils, he loses a standard for excellence *without his realizing it*.

Performing Opportunities: Apart from the local orchestras a teacher should endeavour to form a duo or trio with a pianist and another flute, oboe, violin, guitar or cello. There is an enormous repertoire for the trio sonata and some good modern works too. Churches are a good venue in the early stages to try out repertoire and establish ensemble. It's a great help to pupil and teacher alike when the teacher performs from time to time.

Career Advancement: The best teachers generally have the best pupils. How does a teacher acquire the best pupils?

A teacher whose timetable is filled with a sizeable proportion of pupils who perhaps should have given up, or transferred to another instrument, is not allowing room for a higher proportion of more talented players. It's desirable that there are both teachers and therapists, and mixtures of the two. Only the individual can decide on the correct balance for himself.

If the best teachers generally have the best pupils, more pupils are attracted to them and parents are more anxious that Mary studies with Mr X. The teacher's fees can reflect his popularity and his worth.

Full-Time Teachers: That is to say, those who are fully employed by a local government body, or by a school, are much less free to take decisions about such matters as timetables, fees and pupils. On the other hand, there is security of employment. Some authorities stipulate that part of the timetable of a prospective teacher shall be to take part as a performer in a wind quintet or other chamber music group, and to perform in local schools. It depends on the authority and what funds are available.

Increasingly in recent years, the fully employed and self-employed teachers have had to cope with group lessons, some with as many as ten beginners in a group. The most important point to remember is that to teach ten as productively as one is impossible: each pupil will have different problems and will need a minimal amount of individual attention according to the time available.

A newcomer to the class lesson will be dismayed when faced with so many, but he should bear in mind that though seemingly less efficient, the pupils can learn from each other, and that he will have to devise a method to deal with this new teaching technique, and avoid working himself into a frazzle trying to teach ten as productively as he usually teaches one.

Allied Wind Instrument Teaching: The simple answer to this perennial problem is that flute pupils should be taught by flute players, not bumblephone players. That is an ideal only: in the real world, employers frequently call for flute players to teach at least one of the allied woodwind such as the clarinet, oboe and bassoon. To be idealistic is to reduce one's chances of employment.

The argument against teaching another instrument is that it is impossible to teach adequately an instrument which you cannot play yourself. The facts don't stand up to this. The building blocks of instrumental technique are, in fact, very similar. There are obvious differences of reeds and articulation, but the broad principles are similar. Those who voice the contrary opinion, have usually no knowledge at all of an allied woodwind instrument and are therefore unqualified to pass an opinion. A recent survey of opinion was sought from professors at colleges of music (themselves orchestral players) who were of the almost unanimous opinion that education authorities should employ one-instrument specialists only.

Oddly, the opinions of the *employers* and of the *employed* in education were not sought; they are, after all, the experts!

These building blocks of allied instrument technique can be learned; the teacher's experience on his own instrument will help him to understand the basics of another instrument. The hardest part of teaching – and what it is *really* all about – is the teaching of music, of performance.

Learning the allied instrument is straightforward. It can be learned from a book like this one. Some experience of blowing and articulation is helpful towards a clearer understanding, but a high attainment in performance is not necessary. The eighteenth century tells us a lot: players changed from flute to oboe and sometimes to trumpet and violin as well. The specialist ruined all of that.

Education Authorities simply cannot afford to send a specialist teacher out to a village school to teach one bassoon pupil; they can only afford to send a specialist instrumental teacher *who happens also to teach the bassoon.*

A woodwind teacher should be competent enough to take a pupil at least through the earliest stages without too much harm before passing him on to a specialist in the area – if there is one. It is difficult for a woodwind teacher to find that his clarinet pupil is making really good progress, only to feel the loss at passing him on to a colleague. But the Proper teacher will have the best interests of his pupil at heart.

Which Allied Instrument? To the flute player, the clarinet is the most obvious choice for solely a second instrument, followed by the bassoon.

The clarinet because it is unlikely to interfere with flute playing, and, should a teacher want to blow one, it will cause the least embouchure problems. It is in any case the most popular instrument after the flute. The bassoon is more nearly allied to the clarinet and is an obvious second choice.

It is interesting to note that some fine performers never demonstrate on a flute when *teaching* it. They say it is counterproductive to their own embouchure especially when they have a concert later in the day.

Repair and Maintenance: A Proper teacher – and a Proper player – should acquaint himself wth the mechanical adjustment and maintenance of the flute. Well, that's an ideal. Unfortunately, there are those who have no idea of simple mechanical principles and prefer to 'leave it to the expert'. Some have no natural talent or inquisitiveness about the flute's mechanics and are afraid to experiment lest a ghastly mistake is made. Experts are expensive. The time the instrument is out of use can also be expensive.

The mechanism, though it looks complicated, is easy to understand if some time is given to the study and perusal of the keywork and how it works. The most common problem is that, on pressing one key, a key further away doesn't cover properly. Assuming that the pads are all right and the instrument hasn't been dropped (both problems requiring the expertise of a repair man), the usual cause is either a) the adjusting screws need adjusting; or b) some thin paper needs to be added or removed between the 'clutch' plates.

A simple box of tools should be carried by the Proper teacher to include:

> One screwdriver; an assortment of springs; a small pair of pliers; a small pair of snips; a craft knife; cigarette papers; thin cork; a tube of shellac glue; some goldbeater's skin (for temporarily re-covering a hole in a pad); some elastic bands.

If a flute is going to go out of adjustment, it will do so of course, *just* before the annual School Concert, perhaps only minutes before. There's usually a reason for this: the flute hasn't been oiled for a year or more; when the pupil becomes anxious, his hands get hot and if some mechanical part is to go wrong, it will do so as soon as the instrument becomes warmer than normal.

It's not within the scope of this book to list all the ailments and diseases of mechanical trouble; some books are recommended in the Bibliography.

Beginners' Books: An established teacher will have his favourites. The new teacher will soon discover the most popular methods. Some teachers find that a change of book every three or four years is refreshing. It is worth noting that the flute lends itself most readily to being learned chromatically. It is no more difficult to learn G sharp than G natural. The low register is the fundamental tone of the flute – the second and third octaves are based on the second, third and fourth harmonics. The low register should therefore be given the most attention in the beginning. If this concept is combined with learning all the chromatic notes of the low register, interest is maintained and a firm tonal foundation is laid.*

Studies have been made of the musical preferences of children up to about the age of fifteen. The results show that they most appreciate and enjoy melody and rhythm, not clever counterpoint, harmony or fugue – that may come later.

Whatever *his own* preferences, the Proper teacher will try to interest and inspire his pupils with beautiful melodies and good rhythmic tunes, and encourage them to become familiar with all the key signatures.

*See *A Beginner's Practice Book for the Flute* (Novello).

COMMON PROBLEMS IN TEACHING

Pitch: A person is said to have perfect pitch if they can give the name of any note without having heard a reference note and without attempting to recall any reference note, in other words, without hesitation. This gift is also known as absolute pitch. It is very rare.

Relative pitch is the ability to give the name of any note by momentarily recalling, say, the first note or chord of the *National Anthem*. This gift can be acquired with training, and is quite common. It is often misnamed 'perfect' but is, in fact, *relative* pitch. Someone with perfect, or absolute, pitch could also say whether the given note was in tune, sharp or flat. Many musicians regard perfect pitch as a handicap: in performance, the player may be fingering and blowing a flute which is not producing the exact pitch which he expects. Many 'authentic' orchestras play at low pitch, A = 415 or A = 420.

AN EDWARDIAN POSTCARD

Authorities disagree on whether a person's pitch discrimination can be improved. With the kind of aural training currently in use in schools and colleges, that is, keyboard harmony, interval recognition and modulation, the answer appears to be that it cannot. At the top end of the ability scale, a person can hear differences in pitch of one cent (a hundredth part of a tone). Most, if not all, aural training is based on intervals of a semitone or larger, and it would appear that there can be no hope of a great change in the ability to hear very small pitch changes − as are required when one wishes to play with 'expressive intonation'* − whilst the training is geared to nothing smaller than fifty cents, or a semitone.

This information should be noted well by the Proper teacher, who may be irritated by the pupil who plays badly out of tune. If his pupil can't hear the difference, then the pitch inaccuracy will just have to be accepted. Of course, the problem may not be a mental one, but simply technical which can be improved. The only reliable way is to have the pupil tested to determine what measure of ability he has in pitch recognition. There are some tests available only to musical psychologists, but at least one is available to the general public in music shops.** Many schools use them to select suitable children for instrumental tuition.

Rhythm: Rhythm has been variously defined, the simplest definition being that it is 'the forward flow of music'. A pupil who does not possess a good sense of rhythm is said to be unable 'to predict a given point of time'. This definition is more important to the teacher of beginners.

Rhythm, too, is the lifeblood of music − there can be music without pitch, but none without rhythm. There are many tests of rhythm, each variously claiming to test different aspects of rhythm and rhythmic memory.

The 'ability to predict' is what we need for accurate music making, and the teacher can perform a simple test to indicate broadly any problem with rhythm in his pupil. Firstly, set an accurate metronome to about 100. The pupil should sit comfortably at a table holding a pen or pencil in his hand and tap on the table in time with the ticking metronome. The two 'clicks' should exactly coincide. Then a) the pupil repeats this with his eyes closed; b) the pupil is asked to

*See *Practice Book 6*.
**A. Bentley, *Measures of Musical Abilities* (Harrap).

tap every other click, still with his eyes closed; c) as before, but warn the pupil that you are going to stop the metronome although he must continue tapping *at the same speed*.

After giving many of these tests, the astute teacher will observe that those with a rhythmic weakness tend to tap the pencil in a rather indeterminate and relaxed way; those with a strong sense of rhythm will be very sure about where the next tap should occur and will use their arm and wrist accordingly.

When players have a problem with rhythm, slow pieces are the hardest: they usually become faster. The test c) will clearly show if this problem is present.

These are very simple tests and give a broad guide only as to the degree of difficulty experienced in playing in time. They will do for our purposes, as they can be given, *in situ*, at a lesson.

If a rhythm problem is diagnosed, the pupil should be told that it is still possible to learn to play in time provided he can accept his difficulty. He should be encouraged to do something about improving this important part of music making. A little diplomacy is necessary!

To improve a pupil's ability to play in time, try any, or all, of the following exercises: a) the foot to be tapped in time to all music making (a difficult request if pupils are in the school orchestra or ensemble); b) fit metal 'taps' to walking shoes — the audible click to be used as a basis for humming, or singing other rhythms whilst walking; c) when listening to music, the pupil's fingers should tap out the rhythmic pulse; d) as above but use all the fingers of each hand in turn, to tap out the rhythm heard; e) dancing can be helpful; f) listen for a few moments each day to a clock, watch or metronome and tap the same, and different, rhythms with the fingers, but in time with the 'clicks'.

The involvement of the motor senses — the muscles of the fingers — will help toward an improvement and will make it easier for pupils to play with others and to lead a happier musical life.

Exams and Competitions: There are arguments for and against examinations — especially when the examiner is not a flute player. Why should music be the subject of a marking system? On the other hand, most of what we do is subject to assessment, competition and challenge, so that it is difficult to ignore these factors in teaching. Parents take pride in displaying a certificate of achievement even if it was signed by a deaf, elderly organist who fell asleep during the Mozart Minuet. It is important to remember that the exam syllabus was set up in response to the large majority of teachers. They want exams, even if, for example, the scale requirements are peculiar or inappropriate.

Some teachers prefer to use the exam system as the only means of keeping the interest of the pupil: they progress from one exam to another. Others find different ways of keeping the interest of the pupil. Whichever method, if the pupil responds best to this situation then so be it. The Proper teacher will do what is in the best interests of his pupil.

A LIST OF RECOMMENDED STUDY MATERIAL

Every teacher will have his favourite books which he changes from time to time to alleviate overfamiliarity. I have therefore appended a list of material which is generally recognized as amongst the most important of the books available.

LIST OF STUDIES (ÉTUDES)

Altes	*25 Studies*	Schirmer
Andersen	*24 Studies Op.15*	IMC
	24 Technical Studies Op.63	IMC
Bitsch	*12 Études*	Leduc
Boehm	*24 Caprices Op.26*	Chester
	12 Studies	Leduc
Dick, R	*Tone Development through extended techniques*	Multiple Breath Music Co.
	Flying Lessons	Multiple Breath Music Co.
Drouet	*25 Celebrated Studies*	Schott
Gilbert	*Technical flexibility for flutists*	SMC
Köhler	*35 Exercises Op.33 (3 volumes)*	IMC
Lorenzo	*9 Grande Studies*	Zimmerman
Maquarre	*Daily Exercises*	Schirmer
Moyse	*24 Petites Études Melodiques avec variations*	Leduc
	25 Petites Études Melodiques avec variations	Leduc
	12 Studies after Boehm	Leduc
	Études et Exercises Techniques	Leduc
	Exercises Journaliers	Leduc
	Tone Development through Interpretation	MCA
	50 Variations on the Bach Allemande	McGinnis & Marx
	10 Études d'Après Wieniawsky	Leduc
	12 Studies d'Après Chopin	Leduc
	480 Exercises on Scales and Arpeggios	Leduc
Nicolet	*Pro Musica Nova – Studies for Playing Avant-Garde Music*	MCA
Soussman/ Moyse	*24 Daily Studies*	Leduc
Taffanel/ Gaubert	*17 Daily Exercises and Studies*	Leduc
Wood	*Exercises for Facilitating the Execution of the Upper Notes*	Boosey & Hawkes
Wye	*Practice Books for the Flute*	
	Volume 1 – Tone	Novello
	Volume 2 – Technique	Novello
	Volume 3 – Articulation	Novello
	Volume 4 – Intonation and Vibrato	Novello
	Volume 5 – Breathing and Scales	Novello
	Volume 6 – An Advanced Practice Book	Novello

PICCOLO

Morris & Wye	*A Piccolo Practice Book*	Novello

BEGINNER'S METHOD

Wye	*A Beginner's Practice Book for the Flute, Volumes 1 and 2 and Piano Part*	Novello

A PROPER LIBRARY

Music is an expensive item. In order to minimize costs, the following list should prove useful to the flute player, as it lists the well-known works which most professional players would consider to be 'good' pieces. The range of periods is wide so as to provide a good choice of repertoire.

The list has been graded from A to E to give some idea of the technical difficulty. The inexperienced player should head for E and work his way up to A.

A = difficult   B = quite difficult   C = moderate   D = fairly easy   E = easy

C.P.E. Bach	*Sonata in E*	B	Zimmerman
	Concertos in G, Bb and *D Minor*	A	IMC
	Sonata in A Minor (solo)	C	Ricordi
	Hamburger Sonata	B	Bärenreiter
J.S. Bach	*Sonatas*	B-D	Bärenreiter
	Partita in A Minor (solo)	A	Universal Edition
	Suite in B Minor	A	Breitkopf & Härtel or Schott
	Partita in C Minor	C	Sikorski
J.S. Bach (attrib.)	*Sonata in G Minor*	C	Nagels
Beethoven	*Sonata* (Van Leuwen)	C	Zimmerman
R.R. Bennett	*Winter Music and Summer Music*	B	Mills Music
Berio	*Sequenza I* (solo)	A	Zerboni
Berkeley	*Sonatine*	C	Schott
	Sonata	B	Chester
Blavet	*Six Sonatas*	C-E	Bärenreiter or Muller
Bloch	*Suite Modale*	C	Broude Bros
Boehm	*Du, Du, Liegst Mir am Herzen*	A	Chester (Encores)
	Grande Polonaise	A	Billaudot or IMC
	Nel Cor Piu, and Variation	A	Billaudot
Boismortier	*Suites in B Minor* and *G* (and others)	C	Schott or Bärenreiter
Borne	*Carmen Fantasie*	A	Billaudot
Boulez	*Sonatine*	A	Amphion
Bozza	*Image* (solo)	A	Leduc
Briccialdi	*Carnival of Venice*	B	Allans
Burton	*Sonatina*	B	Fischer
Caplet	*Reverie and Petite Valse*	C	Lemoine
Casella	*Sicilienne and Burlesque*	B	Leduc
Chaminade	*Concertino*	B	Enoch or SMC
Copland	*Duo*	C	Boosey & Hawkes
Corelli	*La Follia*	C	Schott
Couperin	*4th Concert Royaux*	C	Durand or Musica Rara
Czerny	*Duo Concertante*	B	Universal Edition
Damase	*Sonate en Concert*	B	Lemoine
Debussy	*Syrinx* (solo)	D	Chester
Demersseman	*Grande Fantasie on 'Oberon'*	A	Leduc
	6th Solo de Concert	A	Billaudot
Devienne	*Concerto No.8*	B	Boosey & Hawkes
Dick	*Afterlight*	A	Multiple Breath Music Co.

Dohnányi	*Passacaglia* (solo)	A	Broude Bros
Donizetti	*Sonatas in F and C*	D	Peters or Zimmerman
Doppler	*Fantasie Pastorale Hongroise*	C	Chester
	Airs Valaques	B	Emerson
Dubois	*9 Easy Preludes*	D-E	Choudens
Dutilleux	*Sonatine*	B	Leduc
Enesco	*Cantabile e Presto*	B	Enoch
Fauré	*Fantasie*	B	Chester
	Sicilienne (album)	E	Novello
	Morceau de Concours	D	Broude Bros
Françaix	*Divertimento*	A	Schott
Franck	*Sonata*	B	Zerboni
Frederick the Great	*Sonata in A No.12*	D	Sikorski
Fukushima	*Mei* (solo)	B	Zerboni
	Requiem (solo)	A	Zerboni
Ganne	*Andante et Scherzo*	C	Belwin, SMC
Gaubert	*Madrigal*	E	Enoch
	Nocturne and Allegro Scherzando	A	Enoch
Genin	*Carnival of Venice*	B	Chester
Gluck	*Concerto in G Major*	B	Amadeus
	Dance of the Blessed Spirits	E	Schott
Griffes	*Poème*	B	Schirmer
Hahn	*3 Fitzwilliam Sonatas*	C-E	Bärenreiter
	Variations on a Theme of Mozart	C	IMC
Handel	*Sonatas*	C-E	Bärenreiter or Emerson
Haydn	*Sonata in G*	B	IMC
Heiden	*Sonatina*	B	SMC
Hindemith	*Sonata* and *8 Pieces* (solo)	B	AMP or Schott
Honegger	*Danse de la Chèvre* (solo)	C	Salabert
Hotteterre	*Suite in E Minor*	C	Bärenreiter
Huë	*Fantasie*	B	Costellat
Hummel	*Sonata in D*	B	Peters
Ibert	*Pièce* (solo)	A	Leduc
	Concerto	A	Leduc
	Jeux	B	Leduc
Jacob	*Concertos Nos 1 and 2*	B	Boosey & Hawkes
Jolivet	*Concerto*	A	Heugel
	Chant de Linos	A	Costellat
	5 Incantations (solo)	A	Boosey & Hawkes
Karg-Elert	*Sonata Appassionata* (solo)	B	Zimmerman
Kennan	*Night Soliloquy*	C	Fischer
Leclair	*Sonatas in G, C and others*	C	Schott (HM)
Loeillet	*Various Sonatas*	C	Various
Marais	*Les Folies d'Espagne* (solo)	C	Bärenreiter
Martin	*Ballade*	B	Universal Edition
Martinů	*Sonata*	B	AMP
McCabe	*Portraits*	D-E	Novello
Messiaen	*Le Merle Noir*	B-C	Leduc
Milhaud	*Sonatine*	B	Durand
Moscheles	*Grande Sonate Concertante*	B	Billaudot

Mozart	*Concertos in G and D*	B	Novello
	Andante in C	C	Novello
	Rondo in D	C	Heinrichsen
Muczyinski	*Sonata*	B	Schirmer
Nielsen	*Concerto*	A	Dania
Paganini	*24th Caprice (Calimahos)*	A	Schott
Paggi	*Rimembranze Napoletane*	B	Zimmerman
Pergolesi	*Concerto in G*	B	Boosey & Hawkes
Piston	*Sonata*	A	AMP
Poulenc	*Sonata*	B	Chester
Prokofiev	*Sonata*	A	Boosey & Hawkes
Quantz	*Concertos in G and D*	B	Breitkopf & Härtel
	Various Sonatas		
Rameau	*Pieces de Clavecin en Concert*	C	Bärenreiter
Reger	*Romance*	E	Breitkopf & Härtel
Reinecke	*Sonata 'Undine'*	B-C	Universal Edition or IMC
	Ballade Op.288	C	Zimmerman
Rheinberger	*Rhapsodie*	C	Zimmerman
Roussel	*Andante et Scherzo*	C	Durand
	Joueurs de Flute	C	Durand
Saint-Saëns	*Air de Ballet 'd'Ascanio'*	C	Durand
	Romance	D	Durand
Schubert	*Introduction and Variations*	A	Peters, IMC
Schulhoff	*Sonate*	B	Hudební Matice
Schumann	*3 Romances* (album)	D	Novello
Schwindl	*Concerto in D*	B	Breitkopf & Härtel
Seghers	*Souvenir de Gand*	B	Leduc
Silcher	*Variations on Nel Cor Piu*	C	Nagels
Stamitz	*Concerto in G*	B	Schott
Taffanel	*Fantasie on Freyschütz*	A	SMC
Telemann	*Sonatas in F, C and F Minor*	C	Schott
	Methodische Sonatas	C	Bärenreiter
	12 Fantasies (solo)	C	Bärenreiter
	Many other sonatas		
Tulou	*5th and 13th Grand Solos*	B	Billaudot
Varèse	*Density 21.5* (solo)	C	Ricordi
Vivaldi	*Il Pastor Fido*	C	SMC
	6 Concertos Op.10	B	Schott
	Concertos in C and A Minor (Piccolo)	A	IMC
	Concerto in C Minor	B	Editio Musica
Weber	*Sonata in Ab*	B	Eulenberg
Widor	*Suite*	A	Heugel

PROPER PRONUNCIATION

English speaking people are notoriously bad both at learning another language and pronouncing foreign names. The following guide will be useful to those who like to announce their concert items. Firstly, say each composer's name in sections, as indicated, then speed up the delivery. The accented syllable − in italics − is most important if you are to be understood. The letter(s) in brackets are there as a guide; aim for them but don't sound them.

BERBIGUIER	BEAR *BIG*GY AY (AY as in 'HAY')
BERKELEY	*BARK* LEE
BITSCH	*BEE* SH
BIZET	*BEE* ZAY
BLAVET	*BLAH* VAY
BLOCH	BLO(CK in throat)
BOEHM	*BERM* (with lips forward as in OO)
BOISMORTIER	BWA *MORE* TEE YEA
BONONCINI	BON ON *CHEE*NI
BOULEZ	*BOO* LEZ
BRICCIALDI	BRITCH(EE) *AL* DEE
BÜCHNER	BER (with lips forward) KNER (K in throat)
BUSONI	BOO *SEW* NEE
CALIMAHOS	KALEE*MAR*S
CAPLET	*KAP* LAY
CASELLA	KAZ*AY*LA (as in 'hay')
CASTÉRÈDE	KASS TER *RAI*DER
CHAMINADE	SHAMMIN *ARD*
CHERUBINI	KEROO*BEE*NI
CHOPIN	*SHOP* PA(N)
CIARDI	CH(SH)EE *AHR*DEE
COPLAND	*KOPE* LAND
CORELLI	KOR *ELLY*
CORETTE	KOR *ETTE*(R)
COUPERIN	*KOOP*e RA(N)
CUI	*KWEE*
CZERNY	*CHAI*RNEE
DAMASE	DAM *ARZE*
DEBUSSY	DE*BOO* SEA
DEMERSSEMAN	DEM *MAIR*CE MUN
DESPORTES	DAY *PORT*
DEVIENNE	DEV *YEN*
DONIZETTI	DONEE TZETTI
DONJON	*DAW*(N) JAW(N)
DOPPLER	*DOPP* LER
DROUET	*DROO* (W)AY
DUBOIS	DOO *BWAH*
DURAND	DOO *RON*
DUTILLEUX	*DOO* TEE YER
ENESCO	EN *NESS* KO
FAURÉ	*FOR* RAY
FRANÇAIX	FRO(N) *SAY*
FRANCK	*FRO*NK
FÜRSTENAU	*FEAR* STEN OW
GANNE	*GAH*N/GUN
GAUBERT	GO *BEAR*
GEMINIANI	JEM IN NEE *AH*NY
GENIN	*SZJE* NAH
GLUCK	GLOOK (as in LOOK)
GODARD	*GO* DAR

54

GROVLEZ	*GROV* LAY
HAHN	HARN
d'HERVELOIS	DAIR VEL *WAH*
HINDEMITH	*HIN* DER MITT
HOFFMAN	*HOFF* MARN
HOFFMEISTER	*HOFF* MY STIR
HOTTETERRE	*OT* TET TAIR
HUË	OO (with lips forward but 'EE' in mouth)
HUMMEL	*WHO* M'LL
IBERT	EE *BEAR*
de JONG	DER *YONG*
JONGEN	*YONG* GUN
JUON	SZJOO O(N)
KÖHLER	*KER* LER (curler)
KRONKE	*KRONK* E(R)
KUHLAU	*KOOL* OW
LECLAIR	LE(R) *CLARE*
LEMMONÉ	LEM *OWN* AY
LOCATELLI	LOCKER *TELLY*
LOEILLET	*LE*(R) EE AY
LORENZO	LOR *ENZO*
MARAIS	MAR *RAY*
MARCELLO	MAR *CHEL* OH
MARTIN	MAR *TA(N)*
MARTINŮ	*MAH* TEEN OO
MATTHESON	*MATTY* SUN
MENDELSSOHN	*MENDLE* ZONE
MESSIAEN	MESS YA(NNE)
MILHAUD	MEE YO
MINASI	MEE *NA(R)* ZEE
MOLIQUE	MOE *LEEK*
MORLACHI	MORE *LARKY*
MOSCHELES	*MOSH* SHELL ESS
MUCZYNSKI	MOO *CHIN* SKI
NAUDOT	*NO* DOUGH
NIELSEN	*KNEEL* SEN
PAGGI	*PA*(R) JEE
PASCULI	PAS(K) *COOLIE*
PEPUSCH	PEP *PUSH*
PERGOLESI	PAIR GO *LAZY*
PERILHOU	PAIR *EE* YOU
PERSICHETTI	PAIR SEE *KET*TY
PESSARD	PESS *ARE*
PHILIDOR	*FEE* LEE DOOR
PIERNÉ	*PEER* NAY
PIXIS	*PEEX* EECE
PONCHIELLI	PONK *YELLY*
POULENC	*POO* LANK
PROKOFIEV	PRO *KOFF* YEF
PURCELL	PER *SELL*
QUANTZ	*KWUN*TZ
RABBONI	RAH *BONY*
RAMEAU	*RUM* OH
REGER	*RAY* GE(R)
REICHA	*RY* KE(R)
REINECKE	*RI*NE ECKE(R)
RHEINBERGER	*RINE* BEAR GER
RIES	REEZ

RIMSKY-KORSAKOV	RIMSKY-KOR*SAH* KOF
RÔMAN	ROM*AHN*
ROUSSEL	ROO *SELL*
SAINT-SAËNS	*SA*(N) SO(N)CE
SAMMARTINI	SAM MAR *TEENY*
SANCAN	*SO*(N) CO(N)
SATIE	*SA*(R)TY
SAUVLET	*SO* VLAY
SCARLATTI	SCAR *LAT* TEA
SCHICKHARDT	*SHIK* HEART
SCHMIDT	SCH*MEE*(D)T
SCHUBERT	*SCHOO* BAIRT
SCHUMANN	*SHOO* MUN
SCHWINDL	*SHV*IN D'LL
SEIBER	*SJZY* BE(R)
SIBELIUS	SIB *AIL* YOOS
STAMITZ	*SHTAR* MITS
STOCKHAUSEN	*SHTOCK* HOW ZEN
STRAUSS	SHTRO*W*SS
TAFFANEL	TAFFAH *NELL*
TARTINI	TAR *TEE* NEE
TELEMANN	*TAILE*(R) MAHN
TERSCHAK	*TAIR* SHAK/SHUCK
THURNER	*TOUR* NE(R)
VERACINI	VAIRA *CHEEN* NEE
VERDI	*VAIR* DEE
VERHEY	VAIR *HIGH*
VILLETTE	VEE *YET*
VIVALDI	VEE *VAHL* DEE
WALKIERS	*VAHL* KEERS
WETZGER	*VETZ* GER
WIDOR	*VEE* DOOR
WRANITSKY	VRAN *EET* SKI

BIBLIOGRAPHY
AND LIST OF USEFUL PUBLICATIONS

A *Books About the Flute:*

C.P.E. Bach	*The True Art of Playing Keyboard Instruments*	Eulenberg
Anthony Baines	*Woodwind Instruments & Their History*	Faber
Bartolozzi	*New Sounds for Woodwind*	OUP
Philip Bate	*The Flute*	Benn
Theobald Boehm	*Flute and Flute Playing*	Dover
Robert Dick	*The Other Flute*	OUP
Donington	*Baroque Style and Performance*	Faber
	A Performer's Guide to Baroque Music	Scribner
Dorgueille	*L'École Française de Flute*	Editions Coderg
Einstein	*Music in the Romantic Era*	W.W. Norton
H. Macaulay Fitzgibbon	*The Story of the Flute* (1928)	Reeves
R. Galleras	*Histoire de la Flute*	Galleras

James Galway	*The Flute*	Macdonald
Jochen Gartner	*The Vibrato of the Flutist*	Bosse
Hotteterre	*Principles of the Flute, Recorder and Oboe*	Praeger
W.N. James	*A Word or Two on the Flute*	Bingham
John Krell	*Kincaidiana*	Trio Associates
L. de Lorenzo	*My Complete Story of the Flute*	Citadel Press
B.B. Mather	*Free Ornamentation in Woodwind Music*	McGinnis & Marx
	Interpretation of French Music for Woodwind, 1675-1775	McGinnis & Marx
	Making up Your Own Woodwind Ornamentation	The American Recorder
Raymond Meylan	*Die Flöte*	Hallwag
J.J. Quantz	*On Playing the Flute*	Faber
Rien de Reede (ed.)	*Concerning the Flute*	Broekmans & van Poppel
R.S. Rockstro	*The Flute*	Rudall Carte
Rene le Roy	*Traité de la Flute*	Ed. Mus. Trans.
M. Schwedler	*Flöte und Flötenspiel* (1910)	Weber
Roger Stevens	*Artistic Flute*	Highlands Music Company
Nancy Toff	*The Development of the Modern Flute*	Taplinger
	The Flute	Scribner
Christopher Welch	*History of the Boehm Flute* (1896)	Rudall Carte
	Six Lectures on the Recorder	Frowde
H.C. Wysham	*The Evolution of the Modern Flute* (1928)	Conn

B Repair, Maintenance and Construction:

| Albert Cooper | *The Flute* | Cooper |
| J. Phelan and M.D. Brody | *The Complete Guide to the Flute* | Conservatory Publications |

C Catalogues of Flute Literature:

Houser	*Catalogue of Chamber Music for Woodwind Instruments*	Da Capo
James Pellerite	*Literature of the Flute*	Zalo
Bernard Pierreuse	*Flute Literature*	Ed. Mus. Trans.
Franz Vester	*A Catalogue of Flute Music*	Musica Rara
	Flute Music of the 18th Century	Musica Rara
Muramatsu	*General Catalogue of Flute Music*	Muramatsu

D Psychology of Music, and Acoustics:

Arnold Bentley	*Musical Ability in Children*	Harrap
	Measures of Musical Talent (record)	Harrap
G. Revesz	*Introduction to the Psychology of Music*	Longmans
Carl Seashore	*The Psychology of Music*	Dover
C.A. Taylor	*The Physics of Musical Sounds*	EUP

Afterthought: Flautist or flutist? A friend told me he had been at a dinner party when an elderly lady turned to him and said: "And what do you do, young man?" "I'm a flautist", he replied. Some time passed and she suddenly turned to him and said: "What *exactly* is it that you do with floors?"

Perhaps we should try flutist; it's simpler, self-explanatory and widely understood.

It saves awkward questions, too.

INTRODUCTION.

In following the duties of his Profession, the Author has often regretted that so large a portion of the Hour generally devoted to the instruction of a Pupil, should necessarily be occupied in writing down and explaining the best Fingering &c. for particular Passages, and in correcting those bad habits which inexperienced performers are so apt to contract when they have not had the advantage of practising with an able Professor.

His principal inducements, therefore, for publishing the present Work, originated in a wish to save the time of his Pupils, and to meet the wishes of those Amateurs who are desirous of receiving his Instructions, but who, either from distance, or pecuniary disability, are precluded from taking regular Lessons.

The Rules laid down in these PRECEPTIVE LESSONS are not intended for that class of Flute Players who are unacquainted with the common rudiments of an Instruction Book, — but for those who have made some progress on the Instrument.

The Author's chief object will therefore be to elucidate its *Peculiarities* in regard to TONE, FINGERING, ARTICULATION, GLIDING, VIBRATION, and HARMONICS; and he will pay the more attention to these several subjects, because he is not acquainted with any other work wherein they are treated with that perspicuity which their importance to a Finished Performance so justly demands.

The work is intended to be comprised in Twelve Numbers, the first Six of which will illustrate those Keys most generally used and admired; namely, C, G, D, F, B♭, and ♭; devoting a Number to each.

In each Number will be given the Author's best and easiest mode of FINGERING THE SCALE of which he treats; the most perfect and approved SHAKES; — a variety of useful EXERCISES, calculated to facilitate the improvement of the Pupil; — a pleasing SLOW AIR; — and a familiar RONDO.

The last Six Numbers will contain the remaining Major and Minor Keys, and in the arrangement of the Exercises, Airs, and Rondos, of which they will consist, it will be the Author's endeavour to render them as pleasing and attractive as possible, — always preferring to engage the attention of his Pupils with Music of such a character, than to perplex them with difficulties, which even in the hands of the ablest Performers, rather astonish than delight.

Thus, then, without further apology, is this course of PRECEPTIVE LESSONS introduced to the Lovers of this admired Instrument; and the Author has only to hope that the Originality of its plan may not prove its only recommendation.

(NICHOLSON'S Preceptive Lessons Nº 1.)

From Nicholson's *Preceptive Lessons* (1816)

TREVOR WYE

VIDEO

PLAY THE FLUTE
A beginner's guide

TUTORS

A BEGINNER'S BOOK FOR THE FLUTE
Part 1
Part 2
Piano Accompaniment

PRACTICE BOOKS FOR THE FLUTE
VOLUME 1 Tone (plus TONE CASSETTE available separately)
VOLUME 2 Technique
VOLUME 3 Articulation
VOLUME 4 Intonation and Vibrato
VOLUME 5 Breathing and Scales
VOLUME 6 Advanced Practice

A PICCOLO PRACTICE BOOK

PROPER FLUTE PLAYING

SOLO FLUTE

MUSIC FOR SOLO FLUTE

FLUTE & PIANO

A COUPERIN ALBUM
AN ELGAR FLUTE ALBUM
A FAURE FLUTE ALBUM
A RAMEAU ALBUM
A SATIE FLUTE ALBUM
A SCHUMANN FLUTE ALBUM
A VIVALDI ALBUM

A VERY EASY BAROQUE ALBUM, Volume 1
A VERY EASY BAROQUE ALBUM, Volume 2
A VERY EASY CLASSICAL ALBUM
A VERY EASY ROMANTIC ALBUM
A VERY EASY 20TH CENTURY ALBUM

A FIRST LATIN-AMERICAN FLUTE ALBUM
A SECOND LATIN-AMERICAN FLUTE ALBUM

MOZART FLUTE CONCERTO IN G K.313
MOZART FLUTE CONCERTO IN D K.314 AND ANDANTE IN C K.315

SCHUBERT THEME AND VARIATIONS D 935 No. 3

FLUTE ENSEMBLE

THREE BRILLIANT SHOWPIECES